G000122273

Mario Papa Giuliano Iantorno

Famous British and American Songs

and their cultural background

Longman

LONGMAN GROUP LIMITED
Longman House
Burnt Mill, Harlow, Essex.

First edition published by Nicola Zanichelli Editore S.p.A. - Bologna, Italy

Third impression 1981

ISBN 0 582 79088 3

Printed in Singapore by
Huntsmen Offset Printing Pte Ltd

ACKNOWLEDGEMENTS

We are grateful to Mrs Jennifer Manco who kindly revised the material and contributed to the texts, and also to Mr Vittorio Lamberti, Mr Harold Fish, English Language Officer, North Italy, British Council Milan, Mr Paul Altemus, Director of the American Studies Center, Naples, all of whom helped us in our search for suitable songs.
We are also indebted to Mr Alberto Evangelisti, to Mr George Preen, English Language Officer, British Council Rome, to Mr John Anderson, University of Cagliari, to Mr Edward Hackett, Headmaster of St. Faith's School, Wandsworth, London, to Mr Raffaele Ronga, Director of 'Conservatorio di Salerno', and to Mr Alfredo Trombetti, for their useful comments.
Finally we wish to thank all the teachers who have already made use of the material contained in this book and helped us with their criticism and suggestions.
We are grateful to the following for permission to reproduce copyright material:
Box and Cox Co. Ltd., McCullough Piggott and M.C.A. Music, a Division of M.C.A. Inc., for an extract (words and music) from 'Galway Bay' by Dr. Colahan © 1947 Box-Cox (Publications) Ltd., London © 1947 McCullough Piggott Dublin. Copyright renewed. Sole selling agent M.C.A. Music, a Division of M.C.A. Inc. for North, South and Central America. Used by permission. All rights reserved; E.M.I. Music Publishing Ltd., for an extract from 'It's a long way to Tipperary' by J. Judge and H. Williams © 1912 Reproduced by permission of B. Feldman and Co. Ltd; The Essex Music Group for extracts from 'If you are Happy' by Alec Wilder and Tennessee Williams (words and music), 'We Shall Overcome' by Zilphia Horton, Frank Hamilton, Guy Carawan and Pete Seeger (words and music) and 'Little Boxes' by Malvina Reynolds (words and music) published by Tro-Essex Music Ltd., and 'Where Have All The Flowers Gone' by Pete Seeger (words and music) published by Harmony Music Ltd., Warner Bros. Music Ltd., for an extract from 'Blowin' in the Wind' by Bob Dylan (words and music).

CONTENTS

INTRODUCTION

A description of the book

i The songs

This is a collection of thirty-one British and American folk and pop songs. They have been carefully chosen for their artistic and cultural value and for the presence of high-frequency vocabulary and structures. We have also considered the fact that some of the songs are popular but not easily available. Finally, we have tried to select songs which can be sung in chorus and which can be easily grasped by the students because of their catchy tunes.

ii Notes on the songs

A number of notes accompany the songs. They deal with difficulties in vocabulary or with particular aspects of the culture of the English-speaking world. The language used in the notes is strictly controlled and is suitable for students at an elementary level.

iii Reading passages

The content of many songs has been the starting point for the introduction of topics such as the protest song, the peace movements, the housing problem in Britain and U.S.A., etc. The teacher can use these passages as supplementary reading material and for classroom discussion on topics which usually match young people's interests and help them to increase their understanding of British and American life. The linguistic material in these passages is less controlled because they are intended for post-elementary students.

iv Structural index

An index of some of the most common structures included in the songs is available on page 65 so that the teacher can easily find songs which contain the structures he is interested in.

v Suggested procedures for the presentation of songs in the classroom

A general scheme of presentation has been given on page viii. It is not prescriptive, but, we strongly recommend teachers to read it before adopting their own procedures.

vi Exploitation of the songs

Suggestions have been provided so that teachers can exploit the linguistic material contained in the songs.

vii The cassette

All the songs have been recorded on a cassette for classroom use with a cassette-recorder. The tonalities of the songs have been carefully chosen in accordance with the average range of male and female voices, so that the songs can easily be sung, individually or in chorus, by most people.

Basic aims of the book

Songs provide an amusing and relaxing break in the usual routine of classroom activity. They are also the basis for additional classroom practice.
The teacher can use the material of the songs to:
a. introduce new structures in meaningful contexts;
b. reinforce the structures that the students already know;
c. build up vocabulary;
d. revise already known vocabulary;
e. present some of the most important aspects of the foreign culture;
f. practise all of the language skills in an enjoyable way;
g. practise good rhythmical phrasing.

Why introduce songs in the classroom?

Recent researches in the field of foreign language teaching have pointed out that students' motivation and interest are among the most important factors for the learning of a foreign language. There are several means to improve the teaching effectiveness and to raise the interest and motivation of the students. Recorded tapes, filmstrips, sound films, songs, comics, newspapers and magazines are all familiar to teachers and students and they have proved to be, in most cases, very effective because they are strongly related to everyday life. We think that among these teaching aids, pop and folk songs are materials that best reflect young people's concerns as they often relate to important trends in modern society. This is one of the reasons why songs specially constructed for the teaching of particular structures have failed to arouse the students' interest and have often proved to be boring and artificial. Young people enjoy original folk and pop songs because of their authentic cultural content. Moreover, songs can be profitably introduced by all teachers, whatever method they use, and are easily available. We do not claim here that all the problems concerning motivation

can be solved by introducing songs in the classroom, but singing is certainly one of the activities which generates the greatest enthusiasm and is a pleasant and stimulating approach to the culture of a foreign people. Of course, particular attention has to be paid to the choice of the songs. The tunes must appeal to the students, and the musical arrangements must be modern and lively.
Finally, we should not forget that singing is an exceptional teaching tool: in fact, students will take songs outside the classroom and will go on performing them long after the lesson has finished, purely for their own pleasure. Songs are unforgettable. Unlike drills, which usually slip from students minds as soon as they leave the classroom, songs can last a lifetime and become part of one's own culture.

SUGGESTED PROCEDURES FOR THE PRESENTATION OF SONGS IN THE CLASSROOM

These suggestions are not prescriptive and any teacher is of course free to follow the procedures most suitable to him and his class. Anyway, we give here a general scheme of presentation:
i. (Book shut) Give a brief account of the theme or story of the song in the students' own language.
ii. (Book shut) Play the recorded version of the song.
iii. (Book shut) Comprehension questions can be asked at this stage to make sure that the gist of the meaning has been grasped.
iv. (Book open) Read the song and explain the unfamiliar structural and lexical items. Also practise the pronunciation of unfamiliar words.
v. (Book open) The students listen again to the recorded song.
vi. The teacher reads the song line by line, and the students repeat the lines in chorus, in groups and individually.
vii. Play the song several times and invite the students to sing. It often helps if the teacher sings the song and encourages all the students to join in. Sometimes a song is learnt best by singing just the first line, then when that has been mastered, the first and second, then the first, second and third, and so on.
It is up to the teacher to fix the time to be devoted to singing. A whole session can be dedicated to the learning and exploitation of one song or, on the other hand, the whole activity can be spread over a number of sessions, devoting to it only a part of the time.

EXPLOITATION OF THE SONGS

Songs can be exploited in many ways. We give here some examples of exercises we have already used successfully with our classes:

a. Rewriting the lyrics

Once the students have learnt the song, they can try to compose their own verses to be sung to the tune of the song.
One of the difficulties of this exercise is to build up lines which have the same number of syllables as the original ones. Students generally tend to replace the lines of the song word by word, irrespective of the syllables contained in each line. We have found an effective device to avoid this drawback and help the students in their task. They can first write new lines using numbers instead of words. In doing so students become aware of the syllabic structure of the lines.
Here is an example based on *It's a long way to Tipperary.* The lines of the song have been replaced in this way:

One two three four five six and seven
One two three four three four
One two three four five six and seven
Ten eleven sixty-four.

One two ninety-seven
Three four fifty-four
One two three four five and sixty-seven
Three four five two one.

Once this exercise has been done successfully, students can try to replace the numbers with new words, composing in this way a new song which can be sung to the tune of the original one.

Here is an example of new lines written by pupils at an elementary level which can be sung to the tune of *It's a long way to Tipperary.* The exercise was done as group work.

Jack and Susan one day in London
Went to visit the Queen,
But a tall guard near the Palace
Didn't allow them to go in.
But then, from a window,
You can never guess,
'Hello - boys!', cried Betty and Phil together
And they went right in.

b. Sung drills

There are songs which contain sentences or choruses that focus on grammatical patterns and are repeated many times. These songs can be used to practise grammatical items in a lively way.
Here is a list of such songs:

If you're happy
The world must be coming to an end
Three crows
What shall we do with the drunken sailor?
My Bonnie
Glory, glory, hallelujah!
Where have all the flowers gone?
Blowing in the wind
We shall overcome
She'll be coming round the mountain
I'm on my way
When the saints go marching in
He's got the whole world in His hands
Kumbaya
Down by the riverside

c. Sung dramatization

Shanties lend themselves to be used as the basis for a dramatization. As they have a strong rhythm and were originally sung by workmen and sailors to accompany their work, students can sing these songs while pretending to hoist a sail or weigh anchor. A typical sea shanty is *What shall we do with the drunken sailor?* At an elementary level the dramatization of the song can be useful to express, through gestures, the meaning of some actions. *If you're happy* is particularly suitable for this purpose and is always a success.

d. Summary of the song

When the song has a well-defined story, students can be invited to rewrite the story in their own words. Here is a list of songs which can be used for this purpose:

Cockles and Mussels
The wild rover
Clementine
Go down, Moses

e. From direct to reported speech

Some songs are written entirely or in part in direct speech. Students can retell or rewrite them in reported speech.
Songs that best suit this purpose are:

The wild rover
Go down, Moses

f. Dialogue writing

Students can convert the story of the song into a play, creating a dialogue based on what they imagine the characters say to each other, as suggested by the story.
Here are a few songs which lend themselves to this exercise:

The world must be coming to an end
The wild rover
Oh! Susanna
Clementine
Go down, Moses

g. Adding lines

Students can be invited to lengthen some songs by adding new verses singly by inverting one new line. Here is a list of songs which can be used in this way:

If you're happy
The world must be coming to an end
Where have all the flowers gone?
We shall overcome
She'll be coming round the mountain
I'm on my way
When the saints go marching in
He's got the whole world in His hands
Kumbaya

h. Jumbled lines

Identification exercises are possible at an elementary level[1]. Once the students have learnt the song, the teacher writes the lines of the song on the blackboard in a different order. Let us take for example the song *My Bonnie.* The teacher can write the lines in this way:

My Bonnie lies over the sea
Bring back my Bonnie to me
My Bonnie lies over the ocean, etc.

Then, while the class sings the song in the normal line-order, the teacher points to the jumbled lines on the blackboard as they are

1. This exercise has been taken from:
W. R. Lee, *Language teaching games and contests*, Oxford University Press.

sung. Afterwards, students can do the same in turn, identifying on the blackboard the lines as they are sung by the rest of the class. All songs can be used for this recognition exercise.

i. Reconstruction of the song

When the students know the song moderately well, they can try to reconstruct it in two ways:
1. By listening to the sung version on the tape-recorder. During this exercise it is necessary, of course, to stop the tape-recorder after each line, thus allowing the students time to write. The whole procedure should be repeated two or three times.
2. By referring to 'key words'. The teacher should write the most important content words of the song on the blackboard and the students should try to write all the lyrics. In this case you should encourage students to feel that any change in the words of the song is acceptable, provided that the change makes sense and fits the melody.

j. Comprehension and repetition exercise

The verses of some of the songs consist of only one line which is repeated several times. Once the students know the tune, the teacher calls out the first line, and all the class sings the whole verse, as usually happens in a folk concert. This way of singing is useful because it stimulates the students to try to understand and to repeat the line suggested by the teacher so that they can all sing together.
Here are some of the songs which can be sung in this way:

We shall overcome
If you're happy
Glory, glory, hallelujah!
Where have all the flowers gone?
She'll be coming round the mountain
I'm on my way
When the saints go marching in
He's got the whole world in His hands
Kumbaya

k. Project work

Some of the songs can be the starting point for projects. For example, students can research into the following:

Geography
History
Ways of life
Slavery
Wars
Emigration, etc.

It's a long way to Tipperary [1]

(*Traditional*)

It's a long way to Tipperary
It's a long way to go,
It's a long way to Tipperary
To the sweetest girl I know.

Goodbye, Piccadilly! [2]
Farewell, Leicester Square! [3]
It's a long, long way to Tipperary,
But my heart's right there.

1. Tipperary is a little town in County Tipperary in Southern Ireland. The town's main industry is the processing of dairy products. Tipperary became known among the English speaking Allies in World War I because of the song *It's a long way to Tipperary. The soldiers* turned this love ballad into a marching song, and it became one of the best known songs of the war.
2. Piccadilly: one of the most famous squares in London. It is a kind of link between daytime shopping areas and the evening entertainment area. Several important streets meet here.
3. Leicester Square: another famous area for evening entertainment to the east of Piccadilly.

Piccadilly Circus

Piccadilly Circus is certainly the most popular meeting place in London. At its centre presides Eros, a graceful winged archer on the memorial to the Earl of Shaftesbury This monument was the first in London to be made of aluminium. It was designed at the end of the nineteenth century by Sir Alfred Gilbert and has delighted millions of onlookers since its completion. On certain festive occasions people have even climbed the pedestal to embrace the statue.
It is said that the name 'Piccadilly' derives from 'Piccadilly Hall', a house built in the 17th century by a tailor who made 'piccadils' — a kind of high collar with lace edges — hence, popularly, 'Piccadilly'. The house no longer exists.

The statue of Eros in Piccadilly Circus, London.

Cockles and Mussels [1]
(*Traditional*)

In Dublin's fair city,
Where the girls are so pretty,
I first set my eyes on sweet Molly Malone
As she wheeled her wheelbarrow
Through streets broad and narrow,
Crying, " Cockles and mussels, alive, alive-o! "

Chorus:
Alive, alive-o! Alive, alive-o!
Crying, " Cockles and mussels,
Alive, alive-o! "

She was a fishmonger,
But sure 'twas no wonder,
For so were her father and mother before,
And they each wheeled their barrow
Through streets broad and narrow,
Crying, " Cockles and mussels, alive, alive-o! "

Chorus: Alive, alive-o! etc.

She died of a fever,
And no one could save her,
And that was the end of sweet Molly Malone,
But her ghost wheels her barrow,
Through streets broad and narrow
Crying, " Cockles and mussels, alive, alive-o! "

Chorus: Alive, alive-o! etc.

1. A well known Irish folk song. It is a plain story about a girl who sold sea-food in Dublin. The simplicity of the words and the sweetness of the melody, which are the features of this song, reflect the character of the Irish people, who are warm-hearted, friendly and melancholy.
The song is in English, but we know that in Ireland two languages are spoken: Erse or Irish and English. Erse, the old language of the Celts, is spoken mainly among old people in very restricted areas to the west and south-west of Ireland. De Valera, President of Eire, now dead, introduced Irish into Elementary Schools as the only language in which all subjects had to be taught, with the result that children so hated the language that they forgot it as soon as they left school. English is spoken everywhere in Ireland now, but when spoken by the Irish it is softened by a strong ' brogue ' or typically Irish accent.

Dublin and the Irish Free State

Dublin is the capital of the Republic of Ireland and has a population, today, of about 600,000. It was probably founded by the Vikings in the 9th century and was later called Dublin, from the Gaelic words 'dubh' meaning dark, and 'linn', meaning pool. This name refers to the dark waters of the river Liffey which flows into the Irish Sea. Dublin stands at the mouth of this river in a semi-circle round the lovely Dublin Bay and it is the largest port of the Republic, drawing its exports from the whole Republic and being the largest collecting and distributing centre. In the city is the world's largest brewery, Guinness, and its other industries include the manufacture of poplin and linen, biscuits and machinery and there are shipyards, flourmills, railway yards and engineering shops.

Dublin is full of buildings and places of interest. In O'Connell Street, one of the most beautiful streets in Europe, there is the General Post Office building which was the rebels' headquarters at the time of the 1916 Easter Rising. It was here that Patrick Pearse, a poet, barrister, teacher and chosen president of the Provisional Republican Government, and James Connolly, founder of Irish Socialism and a trade union leader, tried, during the week the rising lasted, to control and direct that idealist insurrection. Then the British troops came, and the guns. 450 Irish and 100 British died, the leaders of the insurrection surrendered, and 13 people were executed, including Pearse and Connolly. But during 1919 to 1921, the Irish Republican Army (I.R.A.) waged war on the British Government. This war was ended by the treaty of 1921, which divided Ireland into the Irish Free State (Eire) and Northern Ireland.

Sackville Street (now O'Connell St.), Dublin - Eire. Hulton Picture Library, London

Galway Bay [1]
by A. Colahan

If you ever go across the sea to Ireland,
Then maybe at the closing of your day,
You will sit and watch the moon rise over Claddagh,
And see the sun go down on Galway Bay.

Just to hear again the ripple of the trout stream,
The women in the meadows making hay,
And to sit beside a turf fire in the cabin,
And watch the bare-foot gossoons [2] at their play.

For the breezes blowing o'er the seas from Ireland,
Are perfumed by the heather as they blow,
And the women in the uplands digging praties [3],
Speak a language that the strangers do not know.

For the strangers came and tried to teach us their way,
They scorned us just for being what we are,
But they might as well go chasing after moon-beams,
Or light a penny candle from a star.

And if there is going to be a life hereafter,
And somehow I am sure there's going to be,
I will ask my God to let me make my heaven,
In that dear land across the Irish sea.

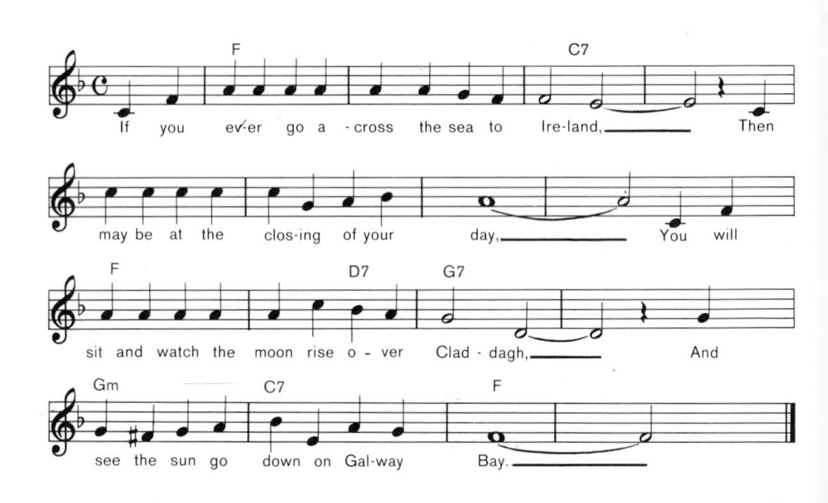

1. Galway Bay: situated on the west side of Ireland, and faces the Atlantic Ocean.

2. Gossoons: children.

3. Praties: Irish dialect for ' potatoes '.

Irish emigration

During the early 1800s, Ireland's population grew rapidly, but its economy, which relied entirely on agriculture, declined. Many people cultivated land but had to pay high rents to the landlords, while others lived on small farms that produced little income. Most of the Irish people had not a great choice for their food and depended mainly on potatoes. But from 1845 to 1847 Ireland's potato crop failed because of a plant disease, and about 750,000 people died of starvation or disease, while hundreds of thousands more left the country and went to the United States which, in those times, represented the ' Promised Land ' for the poor.
So a great movement of emigration began and it went on up to 1921 when Ireland gained its independence, the Germans and the Japanese built new industries, and the Irish improved farming conditions. In America the ' immigrants ' were the people at the bottom of the social ladder: those millions, who had arrived penniless and often illiterate on the crowded immigrant ships, worked in the worst-paid jobs and lived in the worst places. The Irish were the first large group of non-protestant immigrants, and they were desperately poor. In the cities where they went by the thousands, they were always looked upon with suspicion and hostility. But they worked hard and gave their contribution to the growth of their new country.

Emigrants arrival at Cork (Eire). A scene on the quay.

Hulton Picture Library, London

If you're happy [1]

(*Traditional*)

If you're happy and you know it
Clap your hands,
If you're happy and you know it
Clap your hands,
If you're happy and you know it
And you really want to show it,
If you're happy and you know it
Clap your hands.

If you're happy and you know it
Snap your fingers,
If you're happy and you know it
Snap your fingers,
If you're happy and you know it
And you really want to show it,
If you're happy and you know it
Snap your fingers.

If you're happy and you know it
Slap your legs,
If you're happy and you know it
Slap your legs,
If you're happy and you know it
And you really want to show it,
If you're happy and you know it
Slap your legs.

If you're happy and you know it
Stamp your feet,
If you're happy and you know it
Stamp your feet,
If you're happy and you know it
And you really want to show it,
If you're happy and you know it
Stamp your feet.

If you're happy and you know it
Say: 'O.K.',
If you're happy and you know it
Say: 'O.K.',
If you're happy and you know it
And you really want to show it,
If you're happy and you know it
Say: 'O.K.'.

If you're happy and you know it
Do all five,
If you're happy and you know it
Do all five,
If you're happy and you know it
And you really want to show it,
If you're happy and you know it
Do all five.

1. A popular English song for children which is always welcomed by adults, too. While singing it you should dramatize the actions: clap your hands, snap your fingers, etc.

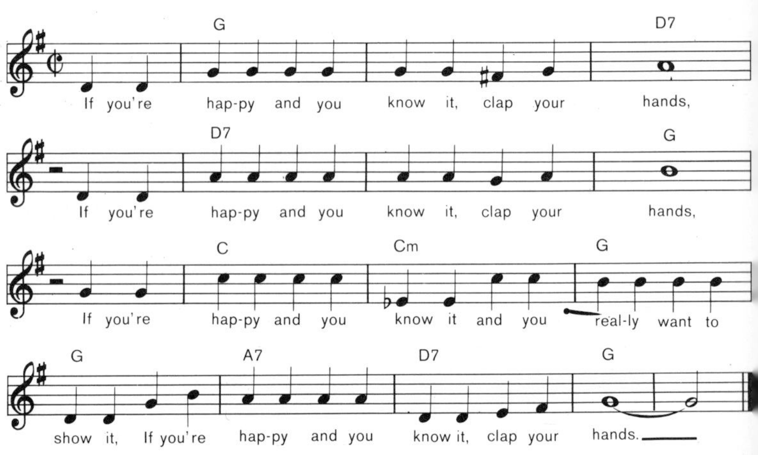

Education

All children in Britain between the ages of 5 and 16 must, by law, attend school or be otherwise educated in a way approved by the local education authority. After the age of 16 a growing proportion are staying on voluntarily at school, some until 18 or 19, the age of entry into higher education in Universities and Polytechnics.
The majority of schools in Britain are supported by public funds, and the education provided is free. But there is also a small sector which includes public schools where parents have to pay fees to send their children. All State schools include primary schools, for children aged up to 11 years (12 in Scotland) and secondary schools. The timetable generally goes from 9.00 a.m to 4.00 p.m. with a lunch break of about 1½ hours. Many students have lunch at school.
Until recently, secondary schools were divided into grammar and secondary modern. During the early 1960s, comprehensive schools were also introduced. Comprehensives are schools where pupils of all abilities are educated together. Many local education authorities are now in the process of changing completely to comprehensive education.

A comprehensive school in Harlow, Essex.

Three crows
(*Traditional*)

Three crows sat upon a wall,
Sat upon a wall,
Sat upon a wall,
Three crows sat upon a wall,
On a cold and frosty morning.

The first crow couldn't fly at all,
Couldn't fly at all,
Couldn't fly at all,
The first crow couldn't fly at all,
On a cold and frosty morning.

The second crow was crying for his ma[1],
Crying for his ma,
Crying for his ma,
The second crow was crying for his ma,
On a cold and frosty morning.

The third crow fell and broke his jaw,
Fell and broke his jaw,
Fell and broke his jaw,
The third crow fell and broke his jaw
On a cold and frosty morning.

The fourth crow wasn't there at all.

1. Ma: short for mother.

The Tower of London and the ravens

The famous Tower of London, first built by William the Conqueror, is often referred to as a place where horrible murders took place. Everybody knows that in the past it was a fortress, a palace and a prison, and from the thirteenth century until 1834 it also housed the Royal Menagerie, the predecessor of the London Zoo.
But ravens are also associated with the Tower where, believe it or not, they are considered special guests. It is probable that there have always been ravens at the Tower, and there is a legend that the Tower will fall if it loses its ravens. The birds are therefore carefully guarded. Six are kept 'on the establishment' and are cared for by a Yeoman Warder. Each bird receives a weekly allowance of 10p. worth of horseflesh, and they have their own quarters in a cage by the Lanthorn Tower. You must not forget that ravens can attain a good age, and one of the Tower birds, James Crow, was a resident for 44 years!

A traditional dweller of the Tower of London.

Hickory, dickory, dock
(*Traditional*)

Hickory, dickory, dock,
The mouse ran up the clock.
The clock struck one,
The mouse ran down,
Hickory, dickory, dock.

Ring a ring of roses
(*Traditional*)

Ring a ring of roses
A pocket full of posies [1]
A-tishoo, a-tishoo [2]
We all fall down.

Sing a song of sixpence
(*Traditional*)

Sing a song of sixpence
A pocket full of rye,
Four and twenty blackbirds
Baked in the pie.
When the pie was opened,
The birds began to sing,
Oh, wasn't that a dainty dish
To put before the king.

The king was in his counting house,
Counting out his money.
The queen was in the parlour,
Eating bread and honey.
The maid was in the garden,
Hanging out the clothes,
When down came a blackbird
And pecked off her nose.

1. Posies: little bunches of flowers.

2. A-tishoo: the sound of a sneeze.

HICKORY, DICKORY, DOCK

D A D A D A D A
Hick-or-y, dick-or-y, dock, The mouse ran up the clock. The
D A G D A7 D
clock struck one, The mouse ran down, Hick-or- y, dick-or-y, dock.

SING A SONG OF SIXPENCE

RING A RING OF ROSES

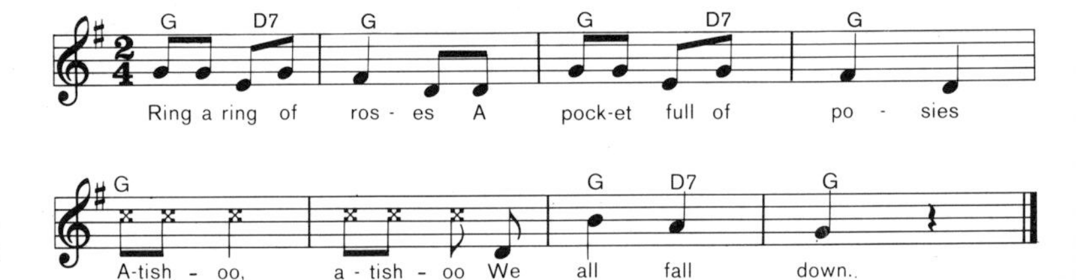

Nursery rhymes

Many nursery rhymes are sung and have thus been included in the repertoire of folk singers. They are distinguished from ballads, love songs and work songs by their humourous and nonsensical contents. Their origin is as ancient as it is obscure. Some, like 'Hickory, Dickory, Dock', are counting rhymes; others, such as 'I gave my love a cherry that has no bone', are riddles; some are lullabies. Some, like 'Sing a song of sixpence', which is supposed to allude to the dissolution of the monasteries by Henry VIII, contain political satire in a veiled form; 'Ring a ring of roses', the English variety of 'Giro giro tondo', is popularly thought to allude to the Great Plague, the roses being the first signs of the illness, 'we all fall down' the inevitable conclusion.

Children in a ring at the public school of Scofield, Utah, in the 1890s. Kansas State Historical Society, (U.S.A.)

What shall we do with the drunken sailor? [1]
(*Traditional*)

What shall we do with the drunken sailor,
What shall we do with the drunken sailor,
What shall we do with the drunken sailor,
Early in the morning?

Chorus:
Hoo-ray, and up she rises,
Hoo-ray, and up she rises,
Hoo-ray, and up she rises,
Early in the morning.

Put him in the long boat until he's sober,
Put him in the long boat until he's sober,
Put him in the long boat until he's sober,
Early in the morning.

Chorus: Hoo-ray and up she rises, etc.

Pull out the plug and wet him all over,
Pull out the plug and wet him all over,
Pull out the plug and wet him all over,
Early in the morning.

Shanties

Shanties, sometimes spelt chanties, are songs with a strong rhythm sung by groups of workmen to accompany their work. Some are sung by miners as they swing their picks against the rock-face, others by lumbermen hauling tree trunks, others by chain gangs working on the roads or the railway. The best known are the sea shanties. These used to be sung on sailing ships to help the sailors haul the anchor chain round the capstan, or pull the ropes that controlled the sails.
Since most of the jobs are now done by machines, shanties have joined the ranks of folk songs. However sea shanties have found their way into the Opera House through the work of the contemporary English composer, Benjamin Britten.

1. Sailors often sang sea shanties when they were working on the ship. In this song, when they say: 'Hoo-ray, and up she rises', they are talking about the big heavy anchor which they are pulling up from the bottom of the sea.

The Inner Harbour, South Quay, Lowestoft (about 1860).

My Bonnie [1]
(*Traditional*)

My Bonnie lies over the ocean,
My Bonnie lies over the sea,
My Bonnie lies over the ocean,
Oh bring back my Bonnie to me!

Chorus:
Bring back, bring back, bring back my Bonnie to me, to me;
Bring back, bring back, oh bring back my Bonnie to me!

Oh blow ye [2] winds over the ocean,
Oh blow ye winds over the sea,
Oh blow ye winds over the ocean,
And bring back my Bonnie to me.

Chorus: Bring back, etc.

Last night as I lay on my pillow,
Last night as I lay on my bed,
Last night as I lay on my pillow,
I dreamed that my Bonnie was dead.

Chorus: Bring back, etc.

The winds have blown over the ocean,
The winds have blown over the sea,
The winds have blown over the ocean,
And brought back my Bonnie to me.

Chorus: Bring back, etc.

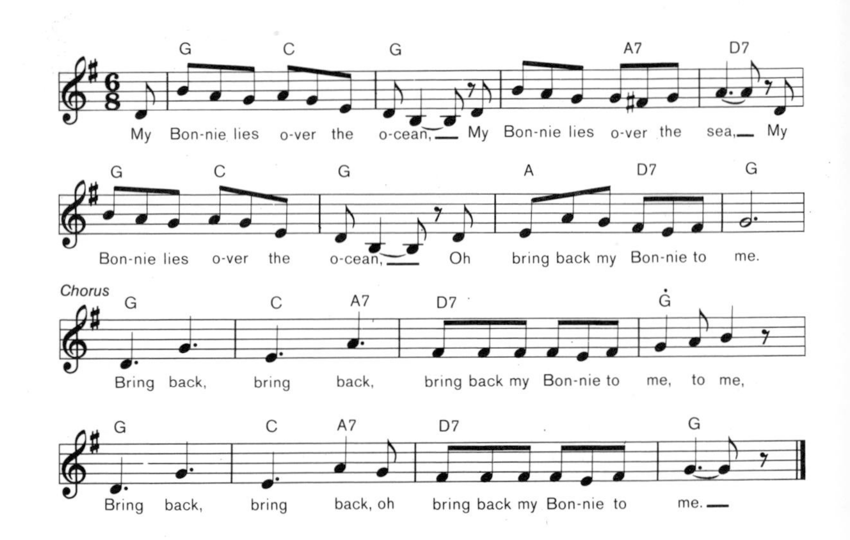

1. This 18th century song from the north of England is an example of a 'chanty'. My Bonnie means 'my loved one'.
2. Ye: an old form of 'the'. If you go to England, you can still see this old word on some signboards of shops and inns, especially in the country. For instance: 'Ye olde pork pie shoppe'.

A nation of sailors

British sailors have helped Britain for centuries, and their contribution to the building of the British Empire as well as to increase the British sea power and fame has been great. Some seamen and ships have become legendary.

Under Queen Elizabeth I, Francis Drake was the most famous of the sea captains and pirates who sailed the oceans. From 1577 to 1580 he voyaged around the world in his ship, ‘ The Golden Hind ’ and he played an important part in the famous battle against the Spanish fleet in the summer of 1588.

In 1869 the ‘ Cutty Sark ’, now preserved in a dry dock at Greenwich, London, and opened to the public, was launched at Dumbarton on Clyde. It was built for the China tea trade, in which there was much rivalry between merchantmen to bring home the first of each new season's tea. The Cutty Sark outdistanced all rivals and proved herself one of the fastest of sailing ships, covering on one occasion 363 miles in 24 hours. Cutty Sark, in Scottish dialect, means ‘ short shirt ’. This curious name was taken from the poem ‘ Tam o'Shanter ’ by Robert Burns where the witch Nannie appeared in a cutty sark. The figurehead of the ship represents Nannie.

One of the most recent great British sailors was Sir Francis Chichester who made his solo circumnavigation of the world from the summer of 1966 to the spring of 1967 in his 53 ft. ketch ‘ Gipsy Moth IV ’, now preserved in dry dock near the ‘ Cutty Sark ’.

Sunday Times, Magnum, Milano

Francis Chichester sailing.

The wild rover [1]

(*Traditional*)

I've been a wild rover for many's the year
And I've spent all my money on whisky and beer;
But now I'm returning with money in great store
And I never will play the wild rover no more.

Chorus:
And it's no nay [2] never,
No nay never no more
Will I play the wild rover,
No never, no more.

I went into an ale-house [3] I used to frequent
And I told the landlady my money was spent.
I asked her for credit, she answered me: " Nay,
Such a custom as yours I can have every day ".

Chorus: And it's no nay never, etc.

I then took from my pocket ten sovereigns [4] bright
And the landlady's eyes opened wide with delight;
She said: " I have whisky and wines of the best
And the words that you told me were only in jest [5] ".

Chorus: And it's no nay never, etc.

I'll go home to my parents confess what I have done
And I'll ask them to pardon the prodigal son,
And when they caress me as oft-times [6] before,
I never will play the wild rover no more.

Chorus: And it's no nay never, etc.

1. The wild rover: a famous traditional British folk song often sung in evening sing-songs at the pub. There are some famous singing pubs in Britain where young and old go to drink and sing together.
2. Nay: no (old use).
3. Ale-house: old name for a public house, in Britain familiarly called a 'pub', where alcoholic drinks are sold.
4. Sovereigns: old British gold coins, face value £1.
5. In jest: as a joke, not seriously.
6. Oft-times: often (old use).

The pub

In Britain people like to meet in taverns, called public houses or more familiarly ' pubs '. There are about 73,000 pubs in Britain and they are more than just drinking houses. Pubs are places where people relax, chat, make friends, sometimes have light meals, play darts and, of course, drink. Most pubs have a dart board and any customer may play. In many pubs there are also dart teams which play matches against teams from other pubs. The most popular drink served in pubs is beer, light or dark. It is generally served in pints, and people drink it either at the bar, that is the counter where drinks are served, or at the tables. There are drinking laws in Britain. By these laws, young people under eighteen are not allowed to buy alcoholic drinks in the pubs, and there are hours during the day when alcoholic drinks cannot be served at all. In fact the usual opening hours for pubs are:

A pub in a suburb of London.

Colin Davey, Camera Press Ltd

London 11.00 a.m. — 3.00 p.m.
5.30 p.m. — 11.00 p.m.

Provinces 11.00 a.m. — 3.00 p.m.
5.30 p.m. — 10.30 p.m. (weekdays)
11.00 p.m. (weekends and public holidays)

Off-licenses (where alcoholic drinks can be bought for consumption elsewhere):
8.30 a.m. until the end of permitted hours.

The world must be coming to an end [1]

(*Traditional*)

I sent her for cheese, oh then, oh then,
I sent her for cheese, oh then.
I sent her for cheese,
But she fell and broke her knees,
Oh the world must be coming to an end, oh then.

I sent her for eggs, oh then, oh then,
I sent her for eggs, oh then,
I sent her for eggs
But she fell and broke her legs,
Oh the world must be coming to an end, oh then.

I sent her for bread, oh then, oh then,
I sent her for bread, oh then,
I sent her for bread
But she fell and broke her head,
Oh the world must be coming to an end, oh then.

I sent her for meat, oh then, oh then,
I sent her for meat, oh then,
I sent her for meat
But she fell and broke her feet,
Oh the world must be coming to an end, oh then.

1. The folk singers Robin Hall and Jimmy Macgregor have picked up this song in the streets of Glasgow. It is an example of the free and easy humour which can be sometimes found in this kind of song.

Glasgow

Although Edinburgh is the capital, Glasgow is the largest city in Scotland and one of the greatest shipbuilding centres in the world. With a population of about 1,000,000 people, Glasgow is also the main centre of commerce and industry. It lies on the river Clyde, which flows into the Firth of Clyde on the west coast of Scotland. Ships, iron and steel and metal goods are Glasgow's most important manufactures. Glaswegians, as the inhabitants of Glasgow are familiarly called, are proud, honest and hard-working, with a characteristic sense of humour. The Scots speak English with a particular accent, and one of the characteristics of this accent is the pronunciation of the letter 'r' with a trill of the tongue.
Glaswegians, like all Scotsmen, like good food and drink. A famous national dish is 'Haggis'. It is made from the heart, liver and lungs of a sheep or calf, chopped with onions, seasonings, suet, and boiled in a bag made from the stomach of a sheep or a calf. Scotland's favourite alcoholic drink is whisky. The Scots have been making whisky since 1400 and they export more than 40 million gallons of 'Scotch' every year.

The Clyde, Glasgow.

Aerofilms, London

Auld lang syne [1]
(*Traditional*)

Should old acquaintance be [forgot
And never brought to mind?
Should old acquaintance be [forgot
And days of auld lang syne?
Chorus:
And days of auld lang syne, [my dear,
And days of auld lang syne,
Should old acquaintance be [forgot
And days of auld lang syne?
And there's a hand, my trusty [friend,
And gi's [2] a hand o'thine [3],
We'll take a cup o'kindness yet,
For auld lang syne.
Chorus:
For auld lang syne, my dear,
For auld lang syne,
We'll take a cup o'kindness yet,
For auld lang syne.

The News Chronicle Song Book gives an easier alternative, 'A smile', which may be sung to the tune of 'Auld lang syne'.

A smile

A smile is quite a funny thing,
It wrinkles up your face,
And when it's gone you'll [never find
Its secret hiding place.
But far more wonderful it is
To see what smiles can do,
You smile at one, he smiles [at you,
And so one smile makes two.

1. This song was originally written by Robert Burns in Scottish. 'Auld lang syne' means, in English, 'old days gone by'. The music was an old Scottish tune. The famous poet, born in Scotland, wrote about three hundred traditional songs, both in the Scottish dialect and in standard English.

People in Britain generally sing this song on special occasions such as New Year's Eve when they gather either at home or in the local pubs and enjoy their glasses of whisky or beer!
2. Gi's: give us.
3. O'thine: of thine; thine: yours (old use).

Robert Burns (1759-1796)

Robert Burns, Scotland's national poet, was born in 1759 at Alloway, in a cottage which now is a Burns museum. Robbie Burns' Night, the date of the poet's birth, is celebrated all over the world by Scotsmen on 25th January.
Burns had a great capacity for love, friendship, and hearty tavern fellowship, and these attitudes provide the chief themes of his poetry. The song 'My love is like a red, red rose' is an example of the poet's qualities.

My love is like a red, red rose

O my love is like a red, red rose,
That's newly sprung in June;
O my love is like the melody,
That's sweetly played in tune.

As fair are you, my bonnie lass[1],
So deep in love am I;
And I will love you still, my dear
Till all the seas go dry.

Till all the seas go dry, my dear,
And the rocks melt with the sun;
And I will love you still, my dear,
While the sands of life shall run.

And fare you well, my only love!
And fare you well a while;
And I will come again, my love,
Though it were ten thousand mile.

R. Burns

1. Lass: girl.

The Scottish poet Robert Burns (after Nasmyth).

Yankee Doodle [1]

(*Traditional*)

Father and I went down [to camp,
A-long with Captain Goodin',
And there we saw the men [and boys
As thick as hasty puddin' [2].

Chorus:
Yankee Doodle, keep it up,
Yankee Doodle Dandy,
Mind the music and the step,
And with the girls be handy.

And there we saw a thousand [men,
As rich as Squire [3] David;
And what they wasted ev'ry [day,
I wish it could be saved.

Chorus:
Yankee Doodle, keep it up, etc.

And there was Captain [Washington [4]
Upon a slapping stallion,
A-giving orders to his men;
I guess [5] there was a million.

Chorus:
Yankee Doodle, keep it up, etc.

And then the feathers on his [hat,
They looked so very fine, ah!
I wanted peskily [6] to get
To give to my Jemima.

Chorus:
Yankee Doodle, keep it up, etc.

1. Yankee is a word generally used for a person coming from the United States.
Doodle means a simple fellow. 'Yankee Doodle' has been popular in America since the colonial days. The tune was popular in Europe during the 1500s and the song was sung to small children in England in Shakespeare's time. Later the tune was used for a rhyme that began:
Lucy Locket lost her pocket,
Kitty Fisher found it;
Nothing in it, nothing in it,
Save the binding round it.
Another English form of the 'Yankee Doodle' tune was sung by the Cavaliers in the 1600s. They made up words to poke fun at Oliver Cromwell when he rode down from Canterbury to take charge of the Puritan forces:
Yankee Doodle came to town,
Upon a Kentish pony.
He stuck a feather in his cap,
And called it macaroni.
At that time the word macaroni was used to mean the young men of London who dressed in odd Italian styles.
The words of 'Yankee Doodle' known in the United States were written by an English army surgeon, Dr Richard Schuckburgh. The song made fun of the untrained American troops during the French and Indian War in 1755. But the American troops liked 'Yankee Doodle' and the song soon became popular. 'Yankee Doodle' was well known all through the American colonies at the time of the Revolutionary War against the English.
2. Hasty Pudding: a thick mess made of boiled corn meal. Although pudding is usually considered to be something sweet eaten at the end of a meal: Christmas Pudding or Chocolate Pudding, it can also be used as a non-sweet accompaniment to meat: Yorkshire Pudding.
3. Squire was a medieval title. It is now used for the local landowner in a country district or village.
4. George Washington was the leader of the American Army which defeated the English during the Revolutionary War (1775-1783). In 1789 he was elected first President of the USA.
5. I guess: in the States it means: 'I think'.
6. Peskily: annoyingly.

Yankee Doodle (Mural by Norman Rockwell). The Nassau Inn, Princeton, New Jersey

American Revolutionary War

The revolutionary war in America was fought by the early thirteen British colonies against Britain from 1775 to 1883, and when the war ended, the thirteen colonies gained their freedom and became the United States of America. Relationships between the colonists and Britain had been good for years, but things began to get worse in 1763 when Britain prohibited the American pioneers from settling and trading in lands west of the Appalachians, because those lands had been reserved for the Indians.

In the following years the British Parliament passed several Acts to tax American goods or goods imported into America, like the Sugar Act, the Stamp Act and the Tea Act of 1773. This last tea taxation provoked a big riot. Some Americans went to Boston harbour where three English ships were waiting to unload tea and organized the famous 'Boston Tea Party'. A band of colonists, disguised as Indians, made their way to the ships, boarded the ships, meeting no resistance, and smashed open 342 chests of tea, dumping all the tea overboard. In the following year the relationship between the Americans and the British got worse and worse, and the war broke out in 1775. The American revolutionary army, led by George Washington, won after 8 years of fighting. The Treaty of Paris in 1783 formally ended the war. In 1776, when the war had already begun, representatives of the North American colonists wrote the Declaration of Independence, setting forth the reasons for declaring their independence from Great Britain.

Glory, glory, hallelujah!

(*Traditional*)

John Brown's body lies amouldering in the grave,
John Brown's body lies amouldering in the grave,
John Brown's body lies amouldering in the grave.
But his soul goes marching on.

Chorus:
Glory, glory, hallelujah!
Glory, glory, hallelujah!
Glory, glory, hallelujah!
And his soul goes marching on.

He's gone to be a soldier in the army of the Lord,
He's gone to be a soldier in the army of the Lord,
He's gone to be a soldier in the army of the Lord,
But his soul goes marching on.

Chorus: Glory, glory, hallelujah! etc.

The stars of Heaven, they are looking kindly down,
The stars of Heaven, they are looking kindly down,
The stars of Heaven, they are looking kindly down,
On the soul of old John Brown.

Chorus: Glory, glory, hallelujah! etc.

American Civil War

The American Civil War, which started in 1861, divided the people of the United States and took more American lives than any other war in history. The four years of bloodshed left a heritage of grief and bitterness that remains in part even today. This war is also called The War of Secession, the War of Independence, but whatever it is called, it was a great turning point in American history. It ended the Southern way of life that depended on slave labour in the cotton and tobacco fields.
Anyway, the slavery issue was not the basic cause of the war, which resulted principally from the economic rivalry between the industrial North and the agricultural South. The major economic groups in the North wanted better tariffs for all their manufactures, free homesteads for farmers and workers, and central banking for merchants and financiers. The South opposed these demands. The result of these contrasts was a bitter war which ended in 1865 after about one million men had been killed or wounded.

John Brown on the scaffold.

John Brown

John Brown lived in the States before the Civil War broke out. He was born in Torrington, Connecticut, one of the Northern States, and spent all his life fighting for the freedom of the Negroes who were kept as slaves in the Southern States. Brown had been considering an invasion of the South, and began to collect arms and men for that purpose. His idea seems to have been to raid the United States arsenal at Harpers Ferry in Western Virginia, and then encourage slaves to rebel. He and 18 followers captured the arsenal on Oct. 16, 1859, but they failed to escape and he was delivered by Colonel Robert E. Lee to the Court for trial. He was convicted on the charge of treason and hanged on December 2, 1859.

Two years later the Civil War broke out, and the Union Troops began to sing ‘ John Brown's body lies amouldering in the grave, but his soul goes marching on ’, to the melody of an old hymn. The American writer Henry David Thoreau (1817-1862) who lived in John Brown's days, wrote in one of his essays: ‘ John Brown did not recognize unjust human laws, but resisted them as he was bid. No man in America has ever stood up so persistently and effectively for the dignity of human nature, knowing himself for a man, and the equal of any and all governments. In that sense he was the most American of us all ’.

Where have all the flowers gone?[1]
by Pete Seeger

Where have all the flowers gone,
Long time passing?
Where have all the flowers gone,
Long time ago?
Where have all the flowers gone?
Young girls picked them every one.
When will they ever learn?
When will they ever learn?

Where have all the young girls gone,
Long time passing?
Where have all the young girls gone,
Long time ago?
Where have all the young girls gone?
Gone to young men every one.
When will they ever learn?
When will they ever learn?

Where have all the young men gone,
Long time passing?
Where have all the young men gone,
Long time ago?
Where have all the young men gone?
Gone for soldiers every one.
When will they ever learn?
When will they ever learn?

Where have all the soldiers gone,
Long time passing?
Where have all the soldiers gone,
Long time ago?
Where have all the soldiers gone?
Gone to graveyards every one.
When will they ever learn?
When will they ever learn?

Where have all the graveyards gone,
Long time passing?
Where have all the graveyards gone,
Long time ago?
Where have all the graveyards gone?
Gone to flowers every one.
When will they ever learn?
When will they ever learn?

1. Pete Seeger, the famous American folk singer and composer, once came across Sholokhov's novel ' And quiet flows the Don ', where he found three lines of an old Ukrainian folk song.
He was favourably impressed by those few lines and tried to find the whole original song. After a year he gave up the search and wrote the words and music of this beautiful song which has become very famous, especially among young people.

Burk Uzzle, Magnum, Milano

Joan Baez in Central Park, New York, singing to a crowd of about 2 000 people.

The protest song

At the beginning of the 1960s there was a great change in the pattern of American and English life. This change was due to the Pop Revolution which broke down social barriers among the young. It was important, especially in Britain, where inhibitions had always given the British the reputation for being cold and reserved. The young broke through their traditional reserve and were no longer afraid of showing their feelings and their thoughts. The Beatles and some American folk singers, musicians and composers such as Pete Seeger, Joan Baez and Bob Dylan, helped the young to break the traditional barriers.
Pete Seeger first gained fame during the 1940s singing about ordinary working people, war, and social problems, and strongly influenced Joan Baez who has always been praised for the simplicity of her vocal style. She, too, like Bob Dylan, saw the changes in society, hated war and the exploitation of black people in America and sang about these ideas.

Blowing in the wind [1]

by Bob Dylan

How many roads must a man walk down
Before you can call him a man?
Yes, 'n' how many seas must a white dove sail
Before she sleeps in the sand?
Yes, 'n' how many times must the cannon balls fly
Before they're forever banned?
The answer, my friend, is blowing in the wind,
The answer is blowing in the wind.

Yes, 'n' how many years can a mountain exist
Before it is washed to the sea?
Yes, 'n' how many years can some people exist
Before they're allowed to be free?
Yes, 'n' how many times can a man turn his head
And pretend that he just doesn't see?
The answer, my friend, is blowing in the wind,
The answer is blowing in the wind.

Yes, 'n' how many times must a man look up
Before he can see the sky?
Yes, 'n' how many ears must one man have
Before he can hear people cry?
Yes, 'n' how many deaths will it take till he knows
That too many people have died?
The answer, my friend, is blowing in the wind,
The answer is blowing in the wind.

1. 'Blowing in the wind' represents a forceful demand for social justice and probably is the best known of all Dylan's songs. In 1964 it became an enormous hit all over the world.

Bob Dylan

Before Dylan it was not so usual that musicians made comments on politics in their songs. Bob Dylan changed this, singing about Vietnam and racial prejudice, and young people came to express their feelings through Dylan's songs. For Dylan words were important, and he wrote songs attacking war, discrimination, exploitation, violence between negroes and white people, and even an angry song, 'A Hard Rain's Gonna Fall', about the dangerous quarrel between America and Russia about Cuba in 1962. 'Blowing in the wind', like most of Dylan's songs, contains political and social ideas, and these ideas are expressed in a simple and direct way, so that they appeal strongly to young people everywhere. And in the 1960s this was especially true in America where many people, especially the young, were beginning to disagree with the American part in the Vietnam war and wanted to make the world a better place to live in, so Dylan became the symbol of protest by young people against what they considered the wrongs of the establishment.

Bob Dylan at the Woodie Guthrie Memorial Concert, 1968.

E. Landy, Magnum, Milano

We shall overcome [1]

(Traditional) - New words and music arranged by Z. Horton, F. Hamilton, G. Carawan and Pete Seeger

We shall overcome,
We shall overcome,
We shall overcome some day,
Oh deep in my heart, I do believe,
We shall overcome some day.

We'll walk hand in hand,
We'll walk hand in hand,
We'll walk hand in hand some day,
Oh deep in my heart, I do believe,
We shall overcome some day.

We shall live in peace,
We shall live in peace,
We shall live in peace some day,
Oh deep in my heart, I do believe,
We shall overcome some day.

We are not afraid,
We are not afraid,
We are not afraid today,
Oh deep in my heart, I do believe,
We shall overcome some day.

Possible additional verses for singing:

We shall all be free, etc.
We will stand together, etc.
Black and white together, etc.
The truth will set us free, etc.

1. It was an old sacred piece, 'I will overcome', which became the anthem of the Civil Rights Movement during the 1930s. We shall overcome' is 'the' song for all people who love freedom. People generally sing it in groups after a song leader who calls out the verses. The song is also the result of the interchange between negro and white musicians in creating American folk music.

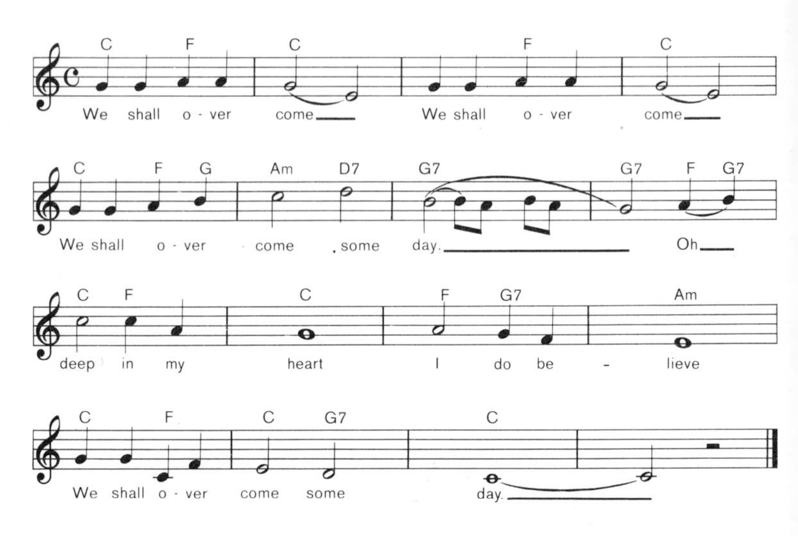

Martin Luther King Jr.: the apostle of non-violence

Martin Luther King (1929-1968), who received the 1964 Nobel peace prize, was the leader of the Negro struggle for equality through non-violent social change. All his life's work aimed at bringing about social, political, and economic equality for Negroes by peaceful means. He preached 'non-violent resistance' to achieve full civil rights for all because he thought that non-violence was the most potent technique for oppressed people. His pleas for non-violence were honoured by the Negroes, despite arrests and troubles of every kind, culminating with the bombing of King's home on January 20, 1956.
His ideas and statements became famous and gave great strength to the movement for Negro freedom. Of segregation, for example, he said, 'Many Negroes unconsciously wondered whether they deserved better conditions. Their minds were so conditioned to segregation that they submissively adjusted to things as they were. This is the ultimate tragedy of segregation. It not only harms one physically, but injures one spiritually'. In his nonviolent protest against injustice, King always tried to instill in his people a sense of dignity and self-respect as well as the right of life and freedom. But violence cut short his life and he was murdered in Memphis, Tennessee, on April 4, 1968.

Martin Luther King speaking to marchers from the steps of the Lincoln Memorial, Washington.

Bob Henriques, Magnum, Milano

Little boxes

Words and music by M. Reynolds

Little boxes [1] on the hillside, little boxes made of ticky tacky [2],
Little boxes, little boxes, little boxes all the same.
There's a green one, then a pink one and a blue one and a yellow
[one
And they're all made out of ticky tacky and they all look just
[the same.

And the people in the houses all go to the university
And they all get put in boxes, little boxes, all the same.
And there's doctors and there's lawyers and business executives
And they're all made out of ticky tacky and they all look just
[the same.

And they all play on the golf-course [3] and drink their Martini dry
And they all have pretty children and the children go to school.
And the children go to summer camp [4] and then to the university
And they all get put in boxes and they all come out the same.

And the boys go into business and marry and raise a family
And they all get put in boxes, little boxes, all the same.
There's a green one, and a pink one and a blue one and a yellow
[one
And they're all made out of ticky tacky and they all look just
[the same.

1. Little boxes is a metaphor for the clean and neat American houses and cottages which are all alike. In this song, however, ' little boxes ' means also compartments, categories.
2. Ticky tacky: trashy material.
3. Golf-course: the area where golf is played. It is a green open area with nine or eighteen holes. A person plays a round of golf when he plays eighteen holes in their correct order. He hits the ball into the holes.
4. Summer camp: nowadays camping is known all over the world as an important source of enjoyment and recreation for many people. In the USA there are summer camps where school departments, colleges and universities send young people for a week or more. Nearly everywhere, camping has become an important business. Millions of dollars are spent each year on hunting, fishing and camping equipment.

The housing problem

The housing crisis in the United States and in Great Britain is a big problem.
The quality of housing in the United States has been improving in recent years, but thousands of families still live in poor, insanitary and overcrowded dwellings. Many Negroes, groups of Mexicans, Puerto Ricans and other immigrants live in these poor areas, called ' slums ', and it is very difficult for these minority groups to improve their conditions because of prejudice and discrimination. In April, 1968, Congress passed a Civil Rights Bill which aimed at eliminating discrimination on the basis of race, colour or religion in the sale or in the rent of most housing.
In Great Britain there are not enough houses, especially in London and other industrial cities. There are still some three million substandard dwellings (houses that do not have inside W.C. or bath or hot water). These slums are being cleared at the rate of 70,000 houses destroyed each year, but a recent development has been for the government to lend people money to convert these city-centre houses instead of destroying them.

Another important contribution to the housing programme was made by the New Towns, built primarily to relieve congestion in the big cities. Most of the new houses built were for families of four to six people with three bedrooms, two living rooms, a kitchen and a bathroom. They are let at a relatively low rent to large families or to those with small incomes. There have also been interesting experiments in tiny flats on the ground floor, or with special lifts for old or disabled people who wish to be independent.

Paul Popper Ltd

G. Berengo Gardin, Ricciarini, Milano

Little boxes, all the same, San Francisco, (U.S.A.) (*above*)

The Negro Ghetto, Haarlem, New York. (*below*)

WESTERN SONGS

The Scots and Irish settled in America at the end of the 18th century, after most of the good land along the Atlantic had been divided among the wealthy families in the New World. So they moved west and settled in the mountains that stretch from the eastern state of Pennsylvania to the southern state of Georgia. They built small farms in the forested valleys and along the sides of rocky hills. They farmed, hunted, cut wood, mined coal, made strong liquor and kept up the musical tradition of their countries of origin. Their songs told stories of ill-fated lovers, of everyday work and problems, with simple lively melodies. It was a music of wild Scottish and Irish dances, and its instruments were chiefly stringed instruments.

The opening of the American West to settlers brought still another change to the mountain song. These songs were created by the cowboy, a man who worked with cattle in the American West. A simple minded man with an earthbound way of life, the cowboy sang songs that were simple in design with little variety in rhythm and melody. He was a lonely man and his songs were filled with a desire for home, a girl and peace from the long day's hard work.

Western and Country music has a quality of sound all its own, a way of singing, and a special feeling for instrumentation. The subject of a song may vary, but you will find in this music a closeness to reality, honesty in dealing with such real life problems as death, love, being poor, but most of all you will find a remarkable sense of humour.

(Adapted from Chapter 5 « Country and Western » in *Popular music* by John Rublowsky, © 1967 by John Rublowsky, Basic Books Inc. Publishers, New York)

Six tenant farmers without farms, Hardman County, Texas, 1938 (U.S.A.).

Oh! Susanna [1]

(Traditional)

I come from Alabama with my banjo on my knee,
I'm going to Louisiana my true love for to see.
It rained all night the day I left,
The weather, it was dry,
The sun so hot I froze to death,
Susanna don't you cry.

Chorus:
Oh! Susanna, oh! don't you cry for me,
I've come from Alabama with my banjo on my knee.

I had a dream the other night
When everything was still,
I thought I saw Susanna
A-coming down the hill.
The buckwheat cake [2] was in her mouth,
A tear was in her eye,
Says I, I'm coming from the South,
Susanna don't you cry.

Chorus:
Oh! Susanna, oh! don't you cry for me,
I've come from Alabama with my banjo on my knee.

1. This song is very famous all over the world; you have probably heard it in films featuring the fabulous Far West.

2. Buckwheat cake: a cake prepared in the States with maize flour especially for breakfast.

Dixieland

Alabama is known as the 'Heart of Dixie'. Dixie or Dixieland U.S.A. Louisiana originally belonged to France and took its name from the King of France Louis XIV. Only later did it become one of the United States.
Dixie or Dixieland is the name often given to the southern States. The explanation for this name comes from the fact that a Louisiana Bank once printed ten-dollar notes bearing the French word 'dix' which in English means 'ten'[1]. According to this story, people called Louisiana 'dix's land', then shortened to 'Dixie' or 'Dixieland'.

Dixie has also another meaning: it is the title of a song written by Daniel Emmett in 1859 which became popular all over the States.
Dixieland is often referred to as the typical rhythmical music played by bands in the States in the early 1900.

A caravan resting in the West.

1. The dollar became the basic unit of money in the United States after the Revolutionary War. The name comes from the old German word ' thal ', which means ' valley '. One of the earliest coins of this type was made in 1519 in the valley of St Joachim in Bohemia and was called ' Joachimsthaler ' and later ' thaler '. The word ' thaler ' was brought to the States by German immigrants, and the English speaking people pronounced it ' dollar '.

Clementine
(*Traditional*)

In a cavern, in a canyon,
Excavating for a mine,
Dwelt[1] a miner, forty-niner[2]
And his daughter Clementine.

Chorus:
Oh, my darling, oh, my darling
Oh, my darling Clementine!
You are lost and gone for ever,
Dreadful sorry, Clementine.

Light she was and like a fairy,
And her shoes were number nine,
Herring boxes without topses,
Sandals were for Clementine.

Chorus: Oh, my darling, etc.

Drove she ducklings to the water
Every morning, just at nine;
Hit her foot against a splinter,
Fell into the foaming brine.

Chorus: Oh, my darling, etc.

Saw her lips above the water
Blowing bubbles mighty fine
But alas! I was no swimmer,
So I lost my Clementine.

Chorus: Oh, my darling, etc.

In a dream she still does haunt me
Robed in garments, soaked in brine;
Though in life I used to hug her,
Now she's dead I'll draw the line.

Chorus: Oh, my darling, etc.

How I missed her, how I missed her,
How I missed my Clementine!
But I kissed her little sister
And forgot my Clementine.

Chorus: Oh, my darling, etc.

1. Dwelt: lived.
2. Forty-niner: Fortyniners were the men who went west in search of fortune during the gold rush of 1849. When gold was found out in California, thousands of people rushed there. They travelled by boat, on foot and on horseback, to reach the gold fields where they hoped to make their fortunes. Towns were built overnight and San Francisco grew from a small town to a city of 25,000 in a year.
Later other gold fields were found out in Colorado as well as in the Klondike district of the Yukon. Not all the people became rich. Many died along the way from cold, hunger, or disease, but some probably made as much as 5,000 dollars in three days.

San Francisco

The city of San Francisco lies on a peninsula between San Francisco Bay and the Pacific Ocean. It is linked to Marin County to the North, through the famous Golden Gate Bridge, and to Oakland, one of the largest cities in California, through the San Francisco-Oakland Bay Bridge, which is more than eight miles long.
In 1848, when the Gold Rush started, San Francisco was a little village with no more than 800 residents. But, since then, many events such as the Gold Rush, the Opening of the Panama Canal in 1914 and World War II have contributed to make this city a place with about 1,000,000 residents. During the years, people from different countries have settled in San Francisco, and the city is now really cosmopolitan. San Francisco has a unique charm of her own, and her two famous bridges as well as the characteristic trams, or cable cars, as they are usually called there, add certainly a lot to this charm. Especially the trams, which are convenient and practical and clang loudly as they transport thousands of passengers daily up and down the steep ascents and discents of this city of hills.

Marka, Milano

Forty-niners at work in a gold field.

She'll be coming round the mountain [1]

(*Traditional*)

She'll be coming round the mountain when she comes,
She'll be coming round the mountain when she comes,
She'll be coming round the mountain,
She'll be coming round the mountain,
She'll be coming round the mountain when she comes.

She'll be driving six white horses when she comes,
She'll be driving six white horses when she comes,
She'll be driving six white horses,
She'll be driving six white horses,
She'll be driving six white horses when she comes.

Possible additional verses:

And we'll all go out and meet her when she comes, etc.
And we'll all have chicken dumplin's [2] when she comes, etc.

1. It is a typical Hillbilly tune, very popular in the States. A Hillbilly is a kind of farmer in the hills. He is usually poor because the land is not very good, and he often lives isolated with his family. This song is also regarded as a tongue twister, that is a phrase difficult to pronounce, especially when it is sung very fast.
2. Dumplin's: dumplings. A dough mixture cooked in broth.

The cowboy

Every European country has its own traditional folktales, but the American past is short and well-documented, so America has very few traditional folktales of her own. But Americans do have the cowboy, and his adventures in films follow the same themes that we find in all folktales: a brave man, with only his horse as a companion, particularly skilful with his pistol and rope, also called a 'lasso', who always fights and wins against evil. Such is the usual hero presented in the movies.
Certainly in the days of the western frontier, cowboys led a dangerous life and worked very hard. They worked on ranches in Texas, Montana, and other western States and they spent long, hard weeks driving cattle from their ranches to railroad towns where the cattle were shipped to the markets of the East. Nowadays life on cattle ranches has changed greatly. Cowboys still use their ropes to catch calves; they feed the cattle and do all the other work but today they use machines for many jobs that earlier cowboys had to do themselves. For example, many American ranchers, in order to search for cattle in the distant parts of the ranch, use helicopters, so life on ranches is no longer lonely and, maybe, has lost the charm of adventure.

A present-day scene out of the past: cowboys drive cattle across the Texas plains. Elliot Erwitt, Magnum, Milano

Marka, Milano

San Francisco, California, 1921: Joseph King Oliver (the third one on the left) playing in what may be considered one of the first official jazz orchestras.

SPIRITUALS

The spiritual is one of the best known forms of American folk music. It is a secular form of hymn, sung at a community gathering or while working in the fields. This explains why it is usually sung in chorus or with a leader.
Spiritual singers often emphasize the rhythm by clapping their hands. The melodies used in spirituals are sometimes said to have come from Africa, have a strong rhythm and are emotional. The origin of spirituals is to be found among travelling preachers, both white and negro, who gathered people in tents, or under the open sky, and spoke to them about the salvation of sinners.
An important part of these meetings was hymn singing. Negroes brought a remarkable musical gift to the singing of the hymns: we must remember that there were not many books of the words or the music of hymns, so improvisation was necessary, and Negroes were exceptionally rich in musical inventiveness and had a deep religious feeling.
Much of the ship loading and plantation work was accompanied by singing of the spirituals. The slaves based most of their spirituals upon characters and stories from the Bible, that is why many of their songs are also called " Gospel songs ".
The manner in which these stories are told in Negro spirituals shows a colourful imagination and a simple faith. Many slaves thought of themselves as the modern children of Israel and looked for a black Moses to deliver them from their bondage. Their songs were warmly appealing and sincere. Among the well-known spirituals are " Go down, Moses " and " Deep River ".

JAZZ

Like so many important musical developments, jazz represents a combination of various musical sounds and rhythms. As jazz developed, it used practically all the melodic and rhythmic sources to be found in America. We can hear traces of religious songs in jazz, old English songs, Negro songs, French dances, and the

rhythm of ragtime (a popular music where the accent of the melody falls just before the regular beat of the accompaniment). We can recognize, too, African instrumental expression, and the rhythms of mountain dances that originated in England. All of these elements were gathered and changed by the Negro to produce that wonderful music we call jazz.
The chief centre for its development was New Orleans, and there was good reason for this. New Orleans, at the time, was known as a fun-loving city where even a black musician might find a job. After the Negro slaves were freed, many found in music a means of earning money. The reasons for this choice are not difficult to understand. First of all, many Negroes were already musicians, and indeed, the Negro musician regularly played music on plantations, the large farms where he worked and lived. Across the South, no important plantation was without a group of black musicians who played at parties. More important, however, was the fact that music provided one of the few areas in which a black man was permitted to excel.
The Negro street bands consisted chiefly of musicians who worked at other trades and played only in their free time. They also learned to play their instruments without any real training. They learned, instead, by a continual process of experimentation. In this way a new kind of performance developed, full of strange sounds that were never taught in any course of study. Very few of these musicians, for example, could read music. They were forced to play by ear. This proved to be a liberating influence. They took familiar songs and melodies and changed them, thanks to an unlimited use of their musical imagination and ability. Gradually, through this kind of personal freedom of expression, a new style of performance developed. Guided only by the feeling and the emotion of the moment, these musicians brought to their music new sound combinations. They also brought the special qualities and devices of Negro singing skills to this music. In their playing, for example, they copied the rough, throaty sounds they used in singing, and in doing this, created a new kind of instrumental tone.
After World War I, American jazz spread abroad. The whole world began to beat its feet to the new rhythms and inventions of musicians from the southern city of New Orleans. Jazz became increasingly popular when Negro musicians were able to put aside their simple musical instruments, sometimes consisting only of a pair of bones, played by hitting one against the other, and obtained traditional manufactured instruments. The range of musical expression was broadened, and this broadened range now demanded a new musical style.
What began as marching bands, soon included ragtime, blues, work songs, and dance music. This expressive, lively, inventive style gradually developed into what became known as Dixieland jazz. The form was developed in Europe, too, and jazz was shaped according to the musical inventiveness of such jazz leaders as Charles Bolden, " Bunk " Johnson, Freddie Keppard, Sidney Bechet and King Oliver. Unlike ragtime, this new jazz was quickly recognized as an important art form.

Giuseppe Pino, Ricciarini, Milano

A great singer of Spirituals and Jazz: Mahalia Jackson.

(Adapted from Chapter 4 « Jazz » in *Popular music* by John Rublowsky,

Nobody knows the trouble I see
(*Traditional*)

Nobody knows the trouble I see,
Nobody knows but Jesus;
Nobody knows the trouble I see,
Glory, Hallelujah!

Oh, nobody knows the trouble I see,
Nobody knows but Jesus;
Nobody knows the trouble I see,
Glory, Hallelujah!

Sometimes I'm up, sometimes I'm down,
Oh yes, Lord;
Sometimes I'm almost to the ground,
Oh yes, Lord.

Oh, nobody knows the trouble I see,
Nobody knows but Jesus;
Nobody knows the trouble I see,
Glory, Hallelujah!

Plantations and slavery

In the Southern States of America, where farming or large plantations formed the main industry, Negro slavery became widespread and profitable. Slave traders from Europe and America caught people in Africa, took them to America and sold them to the southern colonists. The slaves were used in the plantations to raise tobacco, cotton, sugar cane, and to do all the hard work. The cotton plantations needed more and more slaves as labourers because the demand for cotton increased, so in a few years more than 1,000,000 Negroes were carried to America by slave traders.
Life was intolerable for those slaves because slavery often broke up Negro families, separated children from their parents and husbands from their wives. They lived in cabins, the food was scarce, and they received harsh punishment for minor offences. Many laws were directed against free Negroes as well as slaves because the colonists feared that free Negroes might lead revolts.
In 1860 about 4,500,000 Negroes were in the United States and less than 500,000 were freemen. Some had bought their own freedom, but free Negroes often found it difficult to make a living. Most states restricted the kinds of jobs in which a Negro could be employed; white workers in the North often objected to working side by side with Negroes, who were also required to carry passes and could not move about as they wished. There were some movements for the abolition of slavery as well as interesting writings such as Harriet Beecher Stowe's novel, ' Uncle Tom's Cabin ', which focused national attention on the slavery issue, but many years had to pass before slavery was to be abolished.

Picking cotton, Pulaski County, Arkansas, October 1925.

Ben Shahn

I'm on my way
(*Traditional*)

I'm on my way and I won't turn back,
I'm on my way and I won't turn back,
I'm on my way and I won't turn back,
I'm on my way, great God, I'm on my way.

I'll ask my brother, come, go with me,
I'll ask my brother, come, go with me,
I'll ask my brother, come, go with me,
I'm on my way, great God, I'm on my way.

If he won't come, I'll go alone,
If he won't come, I'll go alone,
If he won't come, I'll go alone,
I'm on my way, great God, I'm on my way.

I'll ask my sister, come, go with me,
I'll ask my sister, come, go with me,
I'll ask my sister, come, go with me,
I'm on my way, great God, I'm on my way.

If she won't come, I'll go anyhow,
If she won't come, I'll go anyhow,
If she won't come, I'll go anyhow,
I'm on my way, great God, I'm on my way.

I'm on my way to the freedom land,
I'm on my way to the freedom land,
I'm on my way to the freedom land,
I'm on my way, great God, I'm on my way.

I'm on my way and I won't turn back,
I'm on my way and I won't turn back,
I'm on my way and I won't turn back,
I'm on my way, great God, I'm on my way.

Peace movements

Martin Luther King was not the first man to organize non-violent demonstrations against segregation, racial discrimination and for the freedom of peoples. Many years before, Gandhi had made heroic efforts to free India from British rule and he had employed a variety of techniques, from general strikes to boycotts, marches, massive civil disobedience and passive or non-violent resistance. Luther King organized many demonstrations. In 1963 he led a big march in Birmingham, Alabama, to protest against city-wide racial discrimination, and on August 28 of the same year more than 200,000 people marched after King in Washington, D.C. asking for Negro civil rights. Partly as a result of these mass demonstrations, Congress passed the Civil Rights Act of 1964 and the Voting Rights Act of 1965.
In the 1960s peace groups organized marches and non-violent resistance to demonstrate opposition against U.S. involvement in the Vietnam war and they also called for disarmament and an end to the threat of nuclear war.

Rex Features Ltd

American peace marchers.

When the saints go marching in [1]

(*Traditional*)

Oh when the saints go marching in,
Oh when the saints go marching in,
Oh Lord I want to be in that number,
When the saints go marching in.

Oh when the moon goes down in blood [2],
Oh when the moon goes down in blood,
Oh Lord I want to be in that number,
When the moon goes down in blood.

And when the rebel nation [3] comes,
And when the rebel nation comes,
Oh Lord I want to be in that number,
When the rebel nation comes.

And when the trumpets have to call,
And when the trumpets have to call,
Oh Lord I want to be in that number,
When the trumpets have to call.

Oh when the saints go marching in,
Oh when the saints go marching in,
Oh Lord I want to be in that number,
When the saints go marching in.

Possible additional verses:

Oh when the new world is revealed, etc.
And when the sun begins to shine, etc.
And when the day of judgement comes, etc.

1. This song, which originally was a traditional Protestant hymn, later became one of the most popular ' jazz tunes '. Several versions of this song have been played by great jazzmen such as Louis Armstrong and Lionel Hampton.

2. When the moon goes down in blood: when the moon sets.
3. The rebel nation: the Southern States, that is the slave states, which formed a Confederacy during the Civil War in the United States (1861-1865).

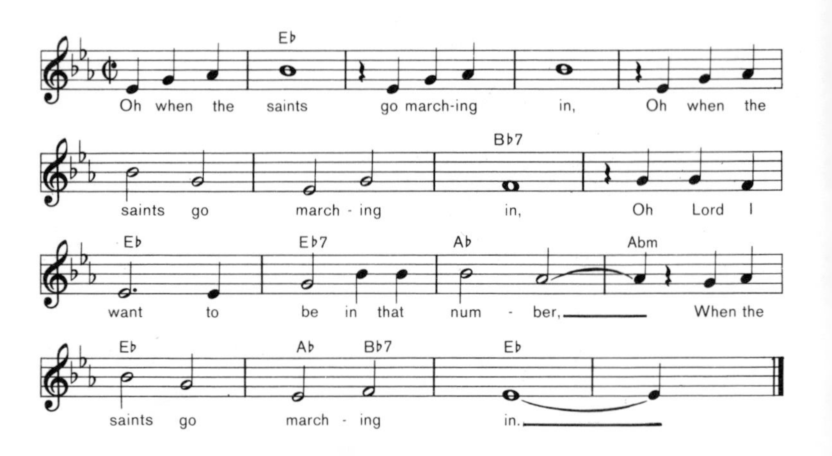

Louis Armstrong

Daniel Louis Armstrong was born in New Orleans on July 4, 1900. His early life was very poor and difficult. When he was 13 he was sent to an orphan's home for boys where he began his life as a musician. In fact the music instructor at the home invited young Louis to join the school band, and Louis played the tambourine, the drums and the bugle. Finally he tried the cornet. The young boy later became the greatest jazzman who has ever lived, a giant among American jazz musicians.
To most people he was just ' Satchmo ', a name he received by accident when a British newspaper editor misunderstood the name ' satchelmouth ' originally given to him because of his large, laughing mouth. But whatever he was called, his trumpet, his grave voice, his ' scat ' singing (the way he used his voice to sing wordless variations on the melody), endeared Louis Armstrong to millions the world over. Because of Satchmo, the style of jazz changed. Not only did his influence bring about a new rhythmic freedom for the performer, but the accent in a jazz performance was now on the soloist instead of on the group. Never before in the history of black music had one individual so completely dominated an art form.
Armstrong's style was copied equally by saxophonists, trumpet players, pianists and all the instrumentalists who make up the jazz picture. Armstrong died on June 6, 1971.

Giuseppe Pino, Ricciarini, Milano

Louis Armstrong.

Go down, Moses
(*Traditional*)

When Israel was in Egypt's land,
Let my people go,
Oppressed so hard they could not stand,
Let my people go,
So the Lord said,

Chorus:
" Go down, Moses, way down to Egypt's land.
Tell old Pharaoh to let my people go ".

So Moses went to Egypt's land,
Let my people go,
He made old Pharaoh understand,
Let my people go,
" Yes ", the Lord said,

Chorus:
" Go down, Moses, way down to Egypt's land.
Tell old Pharaoh, to let my people go ".

" Thus spoke the Lord ", bold Moses said
Let my people go
" If not I'll strike your firstborn dead "
Let my people go
Cause the Lord said,

Chorus:
" Go down, Moses, way down to Egypt's land.
Tell old Pharaoh to let my people go ".

Slavery was one of the causes of Civil War. To most Northerners, the evil was callously compounded in the slave auction, where men and women were bid for like cattle, and families were broken up as their members were sold to separate buyers.

NEGROES
FOR SALE
AT AUCTION
TH'S DAY
AT 1 O'CLOCK

He's got the whole world in His Hands

(*Traditional*)

He's got the whole world in His Hands,
He's got the whole world in His Hands,
He's got the whole world in His Hands,
He's got the whole wide world in His Hands.

He's got you and me, brother, in His Hands,
He's got you and me, brother, in His Hands,
He's got you and me, brother, in His Hands,
He's got the whole wide world in His Hands.

He's got the little bitty babies in His Hands,
He's got the little bitty babies in His Hands,
He's got the little bitty babies in His Hands,
He's got the whole wide world in His Hands.

He's got everybody here in His Hands,
He's got everybody here in His Hands,
He's got everybody here in His Hands,
He's got the whole wide world in His Hands.

He's got my mother and my father in His Hands,
He's got my mother and my father in His Hands,
He's got my mother and my father in His Hands,
He's got the whole wide world in His Hands.

He's got my uncle and my auntie in His Hands,
He's got my uncle and my auntie in His Hands,
He's got my uncle and my auntie in His Hands,
He's got the whole wide world in His Hands.

He's got the birds and the flowers in His Hands,
He's got the birds and the flowers in His Hands,
He's got the birds and the flowers in His Hands,
He's got the whole wide world in His Hands.

Rex Features Ltd

Duke Ellington.

Kumbaya [1]

(*Traditional*)

Kumbaya, my Lord, kumbaya,
Kumbaya, my Lord, kumbaya,
Kumbaya, my Lord, kumbaya,
Oh Lord, Kumbaya.

Someone's crying Lord, kumbaya,
Someone's crying Lord, kumbaya,
Someone's crying Lord, kumbaya,
Oh Lord, Kumbaya.

Someone's praying Lord, kumbaya,
Someone's praying Lord, kumbaya,
Someone's praying Lord, kumbaya,
Oh Lord, Kumbaya.

Someone's singing Lord, kumbaya,
Someone's singing Lord, kumbaya,
Someone's singing Lord, kumbaya,
Oh Lord, Kumbaya.

Kumbaya, my Lord, kumbaya,
Kumbaya, my Lord, kumbaya,
Kumbaya, my Lord, kumbaya,
Oh Lord, kumbaya.

Possible additional verse for singing:

Someone's sleeping Lord, kumbaya, etc.

1. Originally this 'gospel song' was called 'Come by here, Lord'. When it was introduced into the West Indies, however, the natives changed it a little because of the way they spoke English, and the title came to be 'Kumbaya'.
The language spoken in the West Indies is known as 'Creole'. It is a dialect based on English, different from 'Pidgin English'. While Pidgin is only a reduced language useful as a means of communication among people who have no language in common, Creole is a real language spoken by a whole community and learned from birth as the mother tongue.

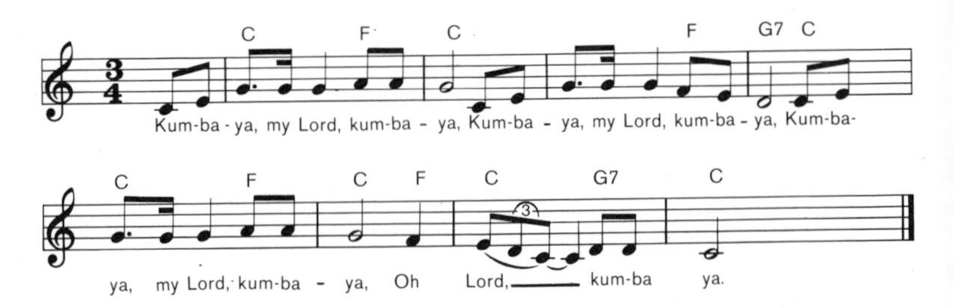

The West Indies

The West Indies are a long chain of islands lying between the Caribbean Sea and the Atlantic Ocean. Once many of them were British colonies, but in the 1960s they became independent and only some remained individually associated with Great Britain. The British government is responsible for their foreign affairs and defence, but the states are self-governing in all other matters. Most of the people in the West Indies are of Negro or mixed Negro ancestry. They work on farms and plantations, but several years ago a lot of them went to Britain to find better jobs. The West Indians are one of the minority groups you notice most in Britain with about one million now living there.

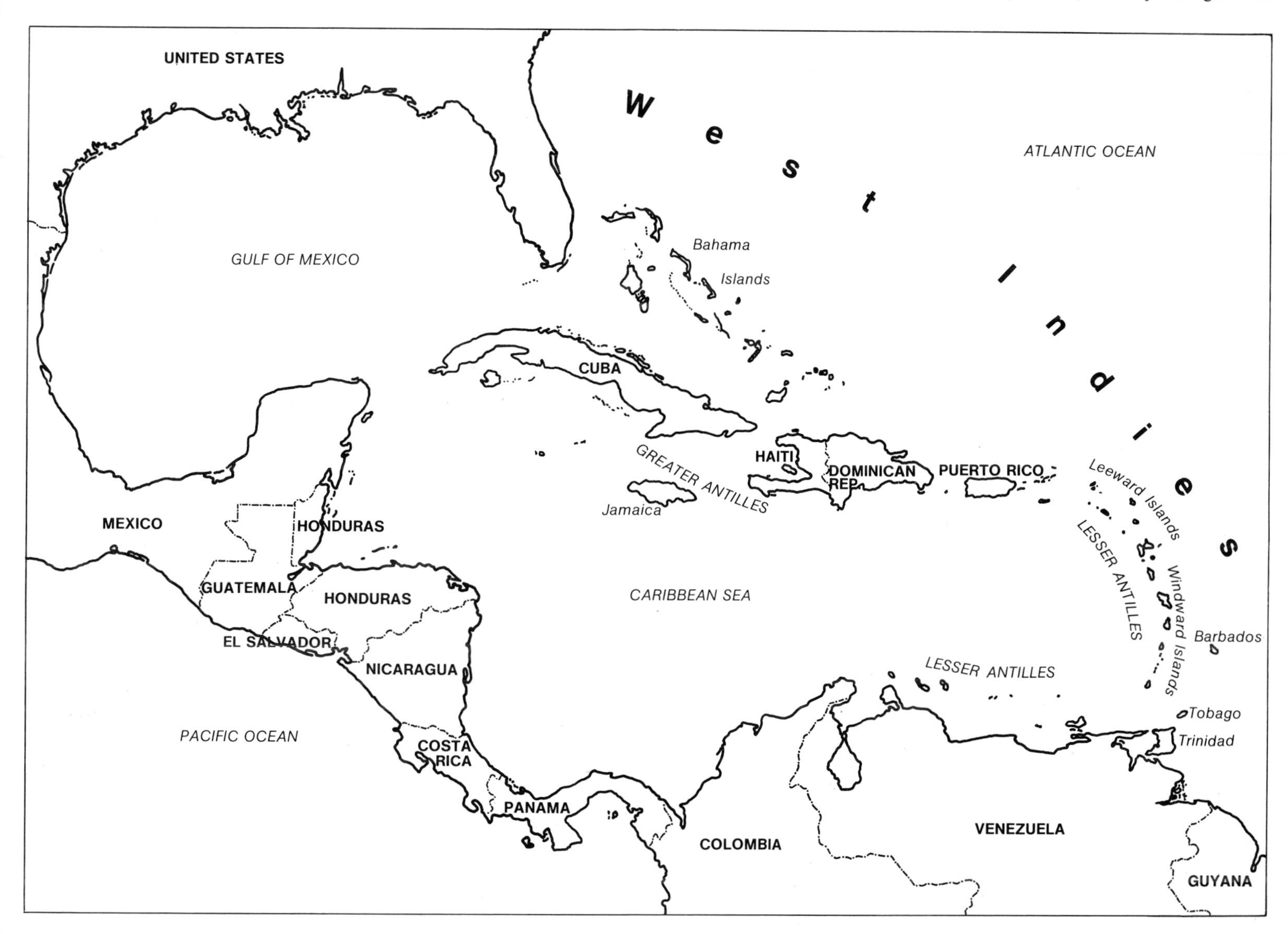
UNITED STATES
West Indies
ATLANTIC OCEAN
GULF OF MEXICO
Bahama
Islands
CUBA
HAITI
DOMINICAN REP.
PUERTO RICO
GREATER ANTILLES
Jamaica
Leeward Islands
LESSER ANTILLES
Windward Islands
MEXICO
HONDURAS
GUATEMALA
HONDURAS
CARIBBEAN SEA
EL SALVADOR
NICARAGUA
Barbados
LESSER ANTILLES
Tobago
Trinidad
PACIFIC OCEAN
COSTA RICA
PANAMA
VENEZUELA
COLOMBIA
GUYANA

Down by the riverside

(*Traditional*)

I'm going to lay down my sword and shield,
Down by the riverside,
Down by the riverside,
Down by the riverside,
I'm going to lay down my sword and shield,
Down by the riverside,
Ain't[1] going to study war no more.

Ain't going to study war no more,
Ain't going to study war no more,
Ain't going to study war no more,
Ain't going to study war no more,
Ain't going to study war no more,
Ain't going to study war no more.

I'm going to lay down my heavy load,
Down by the riverside,
Down by the riverside,
Down by the riverside,
I'm going to lay down my heavy load,
Down by the riverside,
Ain't going to study war no more.

Ain't going to study war no more, etc.

I'm going to lay down my cares and woes,
Down by the riverside,
Down by the riverside,
Down by the riverside,
I'm going to lay down my heavy load,
Down by the riverside,
Ain't going to study war no more.

Ain't going to study war no more, etc.

1. Ain't [eint]: a contracted form of 'is (are, am) not', very common in the USA.

The Mississippi River

The Mississippi River, one of the greatest waterways in the world, is really a milestone in American history. Indian canoes, Spanish vessels, rafts and boats of the early settlers and, later, paddle-wheeled steamboats travelled up and down the Mississippi, exchanging the products of the towns that sprang up along the river banks from North to South.

'Old Man River', as the Mississippi is affectionately known to the millions of people who live along its banks, drains an area which is considered as one of the richest farming regions in the world. For years the floodwaters have brought fertile silt to the Mississippi valley.

The rich history of the Mississippi has given material to poets, novelists, and song writers. You can read a famous description of the river in the book 'Life on the Mississippi', by Mark Twain, a famous American writer who also wrote 'The Adventures of Tom Sawyer'. The Mississippi was also the stage for the colourful Showboat, which was a kind of floating theatre which travelled along the river and stopped in several towns to present stage productions.

The steamboat 'Luella' leaving Leavenworth. The 'Luella' was bound for Weston, Missouri, one of the many small towns dotted along the eastern bank of the Missouri River.

CHRISTMAS

Christmas in London.

Christmas is one of the happiest and busiest times of the year for millions of people all over the world. They observe the holiday with religious ceremonies and prayer. Many people look forward to happy family parties and exchanging gifts. They decorate their houses with holly[1] *and mistletoe*[2]*. Christmas trees sparkle with bright lights.*

In Great Britain, children hang their stockings by the fireplace or by their beds on Christmas Eve, hoping that Father Christmas will fill them with Christmas gifts which they will open on Christmas Day. The British call the day after Christmas, Boxing Day.

Many special songs and carols are sung at Christmas time. Carols are traditional songs of joyful character sung during religious or seasonal festivals such as Christmas, Easter or the month of May. The word "carol" comes from a French round dance called a "carole", and was also used for an English pagan song-dance performed to celebrate the shortest days of winter.

The British are especially fond of "God rest you merry, Gentlemen" and "Silent Night". "Jingle bells" first appeared as a popular song in the United States.

1. Holly: an evergreen tree with green leaves and red berries. The leaves with the berries are used to make attractive Christmas wreaths. In former times, this tree was used in houses and churches at Christmas time, and was called 'holy tree'. The word 'holly' may have come from this name. Nowadays, both in Britain and in North America the holly is used for Christmas decorations.

2. Mistletoe: another evergreen plant used for Christmas decorations not only in Britain and North America but also in Italy and other European countries. It is said that the Druids, the ancient priests of the Celts, cut the mistletoe which grew on the sacred oak and gave it to the people for charms. In many countries, a person caught standing beneath the mistletoe must forfeit a kiss.

God rest you merry, Gentlemen [1]
(Traditional)

God rest you merry, Gentlemen,
Let nothing you dismay,
Remember Christ our Saviour
Was born on Christmas Day,
To save us all from Satan's power
When we had gone astray.

Oh, tidings of comfort and joy,
Comfort and joy,
Oh, tidings of comfort and joy.

In Bethlehem, in Jewry,
This blessed Babe was born,
And laid within a manger,
Upon this blessed morn;
The which His Mother Mary
Did nothing take in scorn.

Oh, tidings of comfort and joy, etc.

From God our Heavenly Father,
A blessed Angel came;
And unto certain Shepherds
Brought tidings of the same:
How that in Bethlehem was born,
The Son of God by name.

Oh, tidings of comfort and joy, etc.

1. This is certainly one of the best known Christmas carols all over Britain.

Christmas Carols

The tradition of singing carols, or joyous songs, at Christmas time is older than Christmas itself. It dates back to pre-Christian times and the mid-winter Yule-tide when an enormous log was burnt ceremonially, accompanied by feasting and drinking and joyous singing. After Christianity was introduced into England, the ceremony was associated with Christmas, the season of hospitality and good cheer. Groups of carol singers go round the houses after dark, guided by the light of a lantern, and sing carols at all the doors. They are often invited in and given mincepies and something warm and alcoholic to drink.
'God rest you merry, Gentlemen, let nothing you dismay' echoes the spirit of goodwill and new hope of the carol singers.

Iced Mince Pie*

Ingredients

1/2 lb mincemeat

1 oz and a half pounds fine sugar

a large lemon

1 oz clarified butter

4 eggs

Method

1. Add to half a pound of good mincemeat an ounce and a half of fine sugar, the grated rind and the strained juice of a large lemon one ounce of clarified butter, and the yolks of four eggs.

2. Beat these well together, and half fill, or rather more, with the mixture, some patty pans lined with fine paste.

3. Put them into a moderate oven and when the insides are just set, ice them thickly with the whites of the eggs beaten to snow, and mixed quickly, at the moment with four heaped tablespoons of fine sugar.

4. Put them immediately into the oven again and bake them slowly to a fine golden brown.

*A small round pastry pie filled with mincemeat (a rich mixture of dried fruit, spices and other ingredients

Jingle, bells! [1]
by J. Pierpont

Dashing through the snow
In a one-horse open sleigh,
O'er the fields we go
Laughing all the way;
Bells on bob-tail ring
Making our spirits bright;
What fun it is to ride and sing
A sleighing song tonight!

Chorus:
Jingle, bells! jingle, bells!
Jingle all the way!
Oh what fun
It is to ride
In a one-horse open sleigh!

1. This very famous song has been translated into many languages and has been sung by many artists including Frank Sinatra and Rocky Roberts.

Bing Crosby and Frank Sinatra

Bing Crosby and Frank Sinatra rank among the most famous singers in the history of popular music.
During the 1930s Bing Crosby started the ' crooning ' style of singing, famous throughout the world. Crooning was the gentle way he used to sing sentimental songs in a narrow range of notes. He won an award in 1944 from the Academy of Motion Picture Arts and Sciences for his performance as a singing priest in the film ' Going My Way '. He died in 1977.
Frank Sinatra, nicknamed ' The Voice ', started out as one of Bing's imitators and rivals and became well-known for both his soulful ballad singing and his interpretations of rhythm songs. He also appeared in about 50 motion pictures, and won the Academy Award in 1953 as best male supporting actor for his work in ' From Here to Eternity '.

Carrese, Milano

Frank Sinatra and Bing Crosby.

STRUCTURAL INDEX

Tenses

Present continuous:

p. 55 Kumbaya:
Someone's crying;
Someone's praying;
Someone's singing;
Someone's sleeping.

17 The wild rover:
I'm returning.

25 Glory, glory, hallelujah!:
They are looking kindly down.

29 Blowing in the wind:
The answer is blowing in the wind.

Present continuous with future reference:

37 Oh! Susanna:
I'm going to Louisiana.

Present simple:

33 Little boxes:
They all go to the university;
They play;
They look the same;
They drink their Martini dry;
The children go to school;
The children go to summer camp;
They come out the same;
The boys go into business;
(The boys) marry and raise a family.

49 When the saints go marching in:
The saints go marching in;
I want to be in that number;
The moon goes down in blood;
The day of judgement comes;
The sun begins to shine;
The rebel nation comes.

29 Blowing in the wind:
She sleeps;
He knows.

7 If you're happy:
You know it;
You really want to show it.

45 Nobody knows:
Nobody knows;
The trouble I see.

13 What shall we do with the drunken sailor?:
She rises.

15 My Bonnie:
My Bonnie lies over the ocean.

Past continuous:

9 Three crows:
The second crow was crying.

Simple past (with regular verbs):

23 Yankee Doodle:
They wasted;
They looked;
I wanted.

39 Clementine:
I missed;
I kissed.

17 The wild rover:
I asked;
She answered;
The landlady's eyes opened wide.

3 Cockles and Mussels:
She wheeled her barrow;
She died of a fever.
5 Galway Bay:
They tried;
They scorned us.
27 Where have all the flowers gone?:
Young girls picked them every one.
37 Oh! Susanna:
It rained all night.
15 My Bonnie:
I dreamed.

Simple past
(with irregular verbs):
39 Clementine:
She drove ducklings;
She hit her foot;
She fell into the foaming brine;
I saw her lips;
I lost my Clementine;
I forgot my Clementine.
37 Oh! Susanna:
The day I left;
I froze to death;
I thought;
I saw Susanna.
17 The wild rover:
I went into an ale-house;
I told the landlady;
I took ten sovereigns;
She said.
51 Go down, Moses:
The Lord said;
Moses went to Egypt's land;
The Lord spoke.
19 The world must be coming to an end:
I sent her for cheese;
I sent her for eggs;
I sent her for bread;
I sent her for meat;
She fell;
She broke her knees;
She broke her legs;
She broke her head;
She broke her feet.
9 Three crows:
Three crows sat upon a wall;
The third crow fell;
And broke his jaw.
23 Yankee Doodle:
I went down to camp;
We saw the men.
5 Galway Bay:
The strangers came.
15 My Bonnie:
I lay on my bed.

Present perfect:
27 Where have all the flowers gone?:
Where have all the flowers gone;
Where have all the young girls gone;
Where have all the young men gone;
Where have all the soldiers gone;
Where have all the graveyards gone.
17 The wild rover:
I've been a wild rover;
I've spent all my money;
What I have done.
15 My Bonnie:
The winds have blown over the ocean;
The winds have blown over the sea;
They have brought back my Bonnie.
37 Oh! Susanna:
I've come from Alabama.
25 Glory, glory, hallelujah!:
He's gone to be a soldier.

29 Blowing in the wind:
Many people have died.

Past perfect:

61 God rest you merry, Gentlemen:
We had gone astray.

Future

The plain future:

47 I'm on my way:
I won't turn back;
I'll ask my brother;
I'll go alone;
I'll ask my sister;
I'll go anyhow.

17 The wild rover:
I never will play the wild rover no more;
I'll go home;
I'll ask them.

31 We shall overcome:
We shall overcome;
We'll walk hand in hand;
We shall live in peace.

41 She'll be coming round the mountain:
We'll all go out;
We'll all have chicken dumplings.

5 Galway Bay:
I will ask my Lord.

51 Go down, Moses:
I'll strike your firstborn dead.

21 Auld lang syne:
We'll take a cup of kindness.

27 Where have all the flowers gone?:
When will they ever learn?

Clauses introduced by *'when, if, etc.':*

41 She'll be coming round the mountain:
She'll be coming... when she comes;
She'll be driving... when she comes;
We'll all go out... when she comes;
We'll all have dumplings... when she comes.

5 Galway Bay:
If you ever go... you will sit.

17 The wild rover:
And when they caress me... I never will play the wild rover.

Continuous form of the plain future:

41 She'll be coming round the mountain:
She'll be coming round the mountain;
She'll be driving six white horses.

The future with *'going to':*

57 Down by the riverside:
I'm going to lay down my sword;
I'm going to lay down my heavy load;
Ain't going to study war no more.

25 Glory, glory, hallelujah!:
He's going to be a soldier.

5 Galway Bay:
There's going to be a life here after.

Imperative:

7 If you're happy:
Clap your hands;
Snap your fingers;
Slap your legs;
Stamp your feet;
Say O.K.;
Do all five.

13 What shall we do with the drunken sailor?:
Put him in the long boat;
Pull out the plug;
Wet him all over.

23 Yankee Doodle:
Keep it up;
Mind the music;.
Be handy.

51 Go down, Moses:
Go down, Moses;
Tell old Pharaoh.
15 My Bonnie:
Bring back;
Blow.

The passive:
29 Blowing in the wind:
It is washed;
They are allowed to be free.
33 Little boxes:
They are made out of ticky tacky;
They all get put in boxes.
5 Galway Bay:
The breezes... are perfumed.
17 The wild rover:
My money was spent.

Be **(Present):**
1 It's a long way to Tipperary:
It's a long way to Tipperary;
My heart is right there.
3 Cockles and Mussels:
The girls are pretty.
7 If you're happy:
If you are happy.
13 What shall we do with the drunken sailor?:
He is sober.
47 I'm on my way:
I'm on my way.
5 Galway Bay:
I am sure.

Be **(Present) To express physical or mental conditions:**
31 We shall overcome:
We are not afraid.

Be **(Past):**
37 Oh! Susanna:
It was dry;
Everything was still;
The cake was in her mouth;
A tear was in her eye.
3 Cockles and Mussels:
She was a fishmonger;
It was no wonder;
So were her father and mother before;
That was the end.
39 Clementine:
Light she was;
Her shoes were number nine;
Herring-boxes... were sandals;
I was no swimmer.
17 The wild rover:
My money was spent;
The words were only in jest.
9 Three crows:
The fourth crow wasn't there.
61 God rest you merry, Gentlemen:
He was born.

Have **(Present):**
17 The wild rover:
I have whisky.
33 Little boxes:
They have pretty children.

Have **(Past):**
37 Oh! Susanna:
I had a dream the other night.

Have got:
53 He's got the whole world in His Hands:
He has got the world in His Hands;
He has got you and me brother;
He has got the little babies;
He has got everybody here.

Do **(As an auxiliary verb):**
5 Galway Bay:
The strangers do not know.

29 Blowing in the wind:
He doesn't see.

Modal verbs

Can:
29 Blowing in the wind:
Before you can call him a man;
How many years can a mountain exist;
How many years can some people exist;
How many times can a man turn his head;
Before he can see the sky;
Before he can hear people cry.
17 The wild rover:
I can have everyday.

Could:
51 Go down, Moses:
They could not stand.
9 Three crows:
The first crow couldn't fly at all.
3 Cockles and Mussels:
No one could save her.

Might:
5 Galway Bay:
They might as well go chasing.

Shall:
13 What shall we do with the drunken sailor?:
What shall we do.

Should:
21 Auld lang syne:
Should old acquaintance be forgot.

Must:
29 Blowing in the wind:
How many roads must a man walk down;
How many seas must a white dove sail;
How many times must the cannon balls fly;
How many times must a man look up;
How many ears must one man have.

19 The world must be coming to an end:
The world must be coming.

Have to:
49 When the saints go marching in:
When the trumpets have to call.

Used to:
17 The wild rover:
I used to frequent.
39 Clementine:
I used to hug her.

Let **(followed by a ' bare ' infinitive):**
51 Go down, Moses:
Let my people go.
5 Galway Bay:
Let me make my heaven.
61 God rest you merry, Gentlemen:
Let nothing you dismay.

Make **(followed by a ' bare ' infinitive):**
51 Go down, Moses:
He made old Pharaoh understand.

Wish **(followed by past forms):**
23 Yankee Doodle:
I wish it could be saved.

Do **used to emphasize:**
39 Clementine:
She does haunt me.
31 We shall overcome:
I do believe.

Say and *Tell*:
17 The wild rover:
I told the landlady;
She said: 'I have whisky'.

Introductory *'there'* **with the verb** *'to be'*:
33 Little Boxes:
There's a green one;
There's lawyers and doctors.
23 Yankee Doodle:
There was captain Washington.

Personal pronouns (object):
17 The wild rover:
I asked her;
She answered me;
You told me;
I'll ask them.
5 Galway Bay:
They scorned us;
To teach us.
13 What shall we do with the drunken sailor?:
Put him in the long boat;
Wet him all over.

Possessive adjectives:
3 Cockles and Mussels:
I first set my eyes;
She wheeled her wheelbarrow;
So were her father and mother;
They wheeled their barrow;
Her ghost wheels her barrow.
39 Clementine:
His daughter Clementine;
Oh my darling Clementine;
Her shoes were number nine;
(She) hit her foot against a splinter;
(I) saw her lips;
I kissed her little sister.
5 Galway Bay:
At the closing of your days;
...the children at their play;
They tried to teach us their way;
I will ask my God;
To let me make my heaven.
17 The wild rover:
I've spent all my money;
I took from my pocket;
I'll go home to my parents.
33 Little boxes:
They drink their Martini dry.

Possessive pronouns:
17 The wild rover:
Yours.

Universal and partitive pronouns and determiners:
3 Cockles and Mussels:
They each wheeled their barrow;
No one could save her.
27 Where have all the flowers gone?:
Where have all the flowers gone;
Young girls picked them everyone.
55 Kumbaya:
Someone's crying.
53 He's got the whole world in His Hands:
He's got everybody here.
45 Nobody knows:
Nobody knows.
61 God rest you merry, Gentlemen:
Let nothing you dismay.

Possessive case:
17 The wild rover:
The landlady's eyes.
25 Glory, glory, hallelujah!:
John Brown's body.
3 Cockles and Mussels:
In Dublin's fair city.

Comparison:

23 Yankee Doodle:
As thick as hasty pudding;
As rich as Squire David.

1 It's a long way to Tipperary:
The sweetest girl I know.

Correlative subordinator

Such...as:

17 The wild rover:
Such a custom as yours.

Plurals (regular):

3 Cockles and Mussels:
Girls;
Eyes;
Streets;
Cockles;
Mussels.

39 Clementine:
Shoes;
Sandals;
Ducklings;
Lips;
Bubbles;
Garments.

19 The world must be coming to an end:
Eggs;
Knees;
Legs.

23 Yankee Doodle:
Boys;
Girls;
Orders;
Feathers.

27 Where have all the flowers gone?:
Flowers;
Girls;
Soldiers;
Graveyards.

5 Galway Bay:
Meadows;
Breezes;
Strangers.

63 Jingle, bells!:
Fields;
Bells;
Spirits.

Plurals (irregular):

39 Clementine:
Herring boxes;
Topses.

33 Little boxes:
Children;
Boxes.

23 Yankee Doodle:
Men.

27 Where have all the flowers gone?:
Men.

5 Galway Bay:
Women.

19 The world must be coming to an end:
Feet.

Numeral ordinals:

9 Three Crows:
The first crow...;
The second crow...;
The third crow...;
The fourth crow....

***One* used as a substitute for a noun:**

33 Little boxes:
There's a green one, and a pink one and a blue one and a yellow one.

Prepositions:

5 Galway Bay:
To, at, of, over, down, on, in, beside, from, by, for, after, across.

3 Cockles and Mussels:
in, on, through, for, of.

9 Three crows:
Upon, on, at, for.

45 Nobody knows:
up, down, to.

39 Clementine:
In, for, without, to, at;
Against, into, above.

13 What shall we do with the drunken sailor?:
With, up, in, out.

37 Oh! Susanna:
From, with, on, to, for;
Down, in.

17 The wild rover:
For, on, with, in, into, to;
From, of.

33 Little boxes:
On, of, out, in, to, into.

25 Glory, glory, hallelujah!:
In, of, down.

63 Jingle, bells!:
Through, in, over, on.

Adverbs:

3 Cockles and Mussels:
First, before.

5 Galway Bay:
Then, just, again, somehow.

45 Nobody knows:
Sometimes, almost.

7 If you're happy:
Really.

25 Glory, glory, hallelujah!:
Kindly.

27 Where have all the flowers gone?:
Ever.

Time expressions:

9 Three crows:
On a cold and frosty morning.

61 God rest you merry, Gentlemen:
On Christmas day.

13 What shall we do with the drunken sailor?:
Early in the morning.

39 Clementine:
Every morning;
Just at nine.

27 Where have all the flowers gone?:
Long time passing;
Long time ago.

31 We shall overcome:
Someday;
Today.

15 My Bonnie:
Last night as I lay on my bed.

Omission of the relative:

1 It's a long way to Tipperary:
The sweetest girl I know.

ALPHABETICAL INDEX

Songs

Reading passages